TW-103

# The Proper Care of
# CATS

**Christopher
Burris**

**Photography:** *Bullock Photography, Isabelle Francais, Dorothy Holby, Robert Pearcy, Fritz Prenzel, Ron Reagan, Dr. Arthur Topilow, and Joan Wastlhuber.*

Distributed in the UNITED STATES by T.F.H. Publications, Inc., One T.F.H. Plaza, Neptune City, NJ 07753; in CANADA to the Pet Trade by H & L Pet Supplies Inc., 27 Kingston Crescent, Kitchener, Ontario N2B 2T6; Rolf C. Hagen Ltd., 3225 Sartelon Street, Montreal 382 Quebec; in CANADA to the Book Trade by Macmillan of Canada (A Division of Canada Publishing Corporation), 164 Commander Boulevard, Agincourt, Ontario M1S 3C7; in ENGLAND by T.F.H. Publications, PO Box 15, Waterlooville PO7 6BQ; in AUSTRALIA AND THE SOUTH PACIFIC by T.F.H. (Australia) Pty. Ltd., Box 149, Brookvale 2100 N.S.W., Australia; in NEW ZEALAND by Ross Haines & Son, Ltd., 82 D Elizabeth Knox Place, Panmure, Auckland, New Zealand; in the PHILIPPINES by Bio-Research, 5 Lippay Street, San Lorenzo Village, Makati, Rizal; in SOUTH AFRICA by Multipet Pty. Ltd., P.O. Box 35347, Northway, 4065, South Africa. Published by T.F.H. Publications, Inc. Manufactured in the United States of America by T.F.H. Publications, Inc.

# t.f.h.

# The Proper Care of
# CATS

**Christopher
Burris**

Before you purchase your cat, you should be aware of local regulations or ordinances regarding the keeping of cats.

# Contents

# Selection and Purchase

The selection of the right cat for you, the owner, depends not on good or bad luck, serendipity, or pity for a serene kitty, but instead on conscious, responsible decisions and planning. It is important that an owner decide if he is ready and able to care for a cat, acknowledging that the continued well being of that animal is placed in his care. Too many persons become new cat owners on the spur (or purr) of the moment, only eventually to abandon the grown-up kitten since

*Opposite:* Some people commence cat ownership with a kitten; others prefer a mature adult feline. **Below:** A beautiful assortment of Himalayan kittens.

*Cats, by nature, are highly inquisitive creatures. Bengals owned by Karen Austin and Tina Woodworth.*

they weren't really prepared for the responsibilities of ownership.

Of all pets in the domesticated world, excepting those kept in a glass bowl or cardboard box, cats are among the easiest to care for, and are practically self-maintaining. The curious and/or perceptive reader thinks at this early point in this handbook, "Well, then why did I buy this book?" Not to fear, Proper Care for Your Cat cannot be achieved by chance, luck or neglect, innocent or simply misguided. Proper care requires understanding the responsibilities and role of keeper, as well as the needs of an animal, and doing your best to meet those needs.

A new owner must begin with a little soul–searching, self-examination, in order to determine the reasons he wants to own a cat, or be owned by a cat, as the case may be. Commitment of time and money, and the expenditure of energy accompany ownership and an owner must be ready to devote all of these in order to accommodate the cat properly. For the dedicated cat person, caring for an animal is not a chore, or a series of tedious daily tasks;

instead it is quality time invested in an affectionate, living creature. The affection of a cat, its heartfelt devotion rubbed against a person's leg, makes keeping that animal a special part of life. Cat owners most usually remain cat owners and cannot see their lives as complete without at least one feline inhabiting their abode.

Since cats are basically small (domestic cats, that is), living quarters do not pose too much of a consideration. Cats belong indoors, and your house or apartment must be large enough to allow the cat enough space to dwell. City cats fend well enough sharing a studio apartment with a loving owner; thus space isn't much of a trouble spot.

Finances must be considered, but cannot take precedence over an owner's decision. That a person can afford a cat is no reason to keep a cat, and the reverse may also be true. Maintaining a single cat is a rather economical

*Contrary to popular opinion, cats and dogs are not natural enemies. If raised together from an early age, they can be great pals.*

undertaking and money doesn't figure into the ultimate decision. On the other hand, initiating a breeding program for purebred cats does require a great deal of money, as well as knowledge and commitment. We do not intend to discuss such an industrious undertaking in this book, but will focus instead on the person who desires to keep one or a few cats in his home as pets.

*These Siamese kits already exhibit the unique charm of their breed.*

Once you have decided that a cat will enhance your life, that you can properly dedicate time to the animal, and that your lifestyle is amenable to a feline addition, you can begin to examine the various possibilities which the cat world has to offer. Cats are all similar in size, though they vary tremendously in color, character, facial expression, and coats. Consider also whether an adult cat or a kitten suits your needs, male or female, one cat or more, purebred or mixed breed, and the importance of pedigree quality.

There are so noteworthy, often overlooked, virtues to adopting a mature cat. Adult cats are arguably adaptable and good-natured. If the cat has been well trained and well taken care of, you can find a quality companion in a flash by selecting the adult. Additionally, adults already

*Classic elegance is embodied in the Oriental Shorthair.*

***Above:*** *You can be sure that your feline friend will get into just about everything in your home, if he is given the opportunity.* ***Opposite:*** *Silver tabby American Shorthair.*

understand their role in the human world and are easier to maintain. Single persons who work for the larger portion of the day may opt for an adult since it is able to spend a day alone with little complaint or difficulty. Adults can also mouse and free a residence from rodents in a jiffy—should an owner need an exterminator right away. Kittens, on the other

hand, need constant attention and supervision. Their curiosity and frailty make them as vulnerable to harm. But, yes, kittens are fun, and a family can learn about the cat's personality by watching it grow up. A home with children properly instructed and supervised, welcomes a kitten with open arms. Time is of the essence, the commitment of countless

***Opposite:*** *Holiday season activities should not interfere with your cat's daily routine.* ***Above:*** *The lovely Snowshoe, one of the newer breeds of cat.*

hours with a kitten, training and teaching it the family ropes.

The choice of male or female, tom or queen, is no royal problem and mostly a matter of personal preference. For persons who do not intend to breed their cat or show their cat, male versus female is even less important. Pet cats, practically without exception, should be altered. Spaying and castration simplifies life with a pet cat,

**Left:** An attractive mixed breed.
**Opposite:** To avoid damage to household items, "cat-proof" your home.

relieving tom owners of putridly stained carpets and long hours listening to the cat arpeggiate in half-tones and queen owners of a straying, unexpectedly impregnated cat, mood swings (?), and also putridly stained carpets. Neutered cats are no less cats, intact with their prey instincts and more focused or consistent in general. They also stray less and are more interested in the human species. The horrendous overpopulation of cats and the millions euthanized annually must convince owners to do their part and lessen the number of cats without homes and proper food.

On to the question of one cat or more: an owner should not feel compelled to keep two cats to help diminish the overpopulation problem. Your personal situation will warrant the affordability and feasibility of keeping two or more cats. Not all felines are social creatures, and many prefer not to be in the company of their own kind. Other cats thrive on cat companionship and prefer it to human attention, except at meal times. Acquiring two kittens at the same time oftimes works out well, since acquainting an adult to a newly acquired kitten can be

*Every cat is an individual with a personality all its own.*

to pass the hours until you get home to clean up the mess. Some owners have experienced that having two cats relinquished both cats' attention for the owner. The truth of this supposition cannot be proven or disproved since cats vary so substantially from breed to breed and individual to individual.

The world of show cats and purebred cats makes choosing a cat breed a stirring adventure. There are nearly fifty cat breeds from which to choose; each one is different, offering a new turn on the cat theme. Before submersing ourselves into that multi-colored, multi-nationality pool, we can also consider the possibility of adopting an average "tom " (or queen). Mixed breed or mongrel cats comprise the largest portion of the cat population in every country in the world. Alley cats, street cats, and household

problematic. Feline bonding is an important consideration, especially for the owner who spends many hours away from home. Two cats, deep in feline like, will find new and exciting ways

*For some fanciers, nothing beats the thrill of show competition. Chartreux owned by Debbie Rexelle.*

pets comprise the group of mongrels (that is not to say that a purebred cat cannot take to the alleys, streets, or households, of course). Acknowledging the multitude of homeless cats, most of whom are mixed breeds, an owner can seriously contemplate adopting such a cat from a shelter. While this is an economically painless venture, other considerations must be stressed. The health of a mongrel cannot be trusted, since in most cases the breeder, parents, and medical history do not accompany the purchase. Before bringing such a cat into your home, visit your veterinarian for immunizations and a general

*You should be fully aware of all the responsibilities of cat ownership before you purchase a cat.*

*An assortment of Siamese. This breed, without doubt, is one of the most popular breeds of cat.*

check-up. Upon the vet's advice, you can determine the soundness of the animal's health and the likelihood of its continued hardiness.

If you wish, however, to acquire a specific kind of cat, it is time to dive into the pool of purebreds and pedigrees. There are two types of purebred cats, show-quality and pet-quality.

Show-quality cats are those animals which are near-perfect in physical make-up and come from lines of champion pedigrees. Pet-quality cats, from those same purebred lines, are those animals that do not shine through in breed type. The flaws of a pet-quality purebred cannot be noticed by a novice, but can be

*Kitten on the keys . . .Able and agile, felines will explore every nook and cranny.*

recognized by a show judge or experienced breeders. Both show and pet quality cats should be healthy and hardy in every way. Persons who desire to show or breed their cat need to purchase a show-quality (or breeder-quality) cat. Pet-quality purebreds should not be bred and, although they can be exhibited, are not likely to compete well against show-quality cats. The price of a show-quality or breeder-quality cat is substantially higher than a pet-quality cat. Most breeders will not permit their top cats to enter homes where they will live only as pets; likewise, breeders will not encourage owners of pet-quality purebreds to enter the show ring. In both cases, the reputation and betterment of a breeder's lines cannot be served. An owner's determination thus rests on his intentions for his cat. If you wish to show or breed your cat, you are ill-advised to shop for the best prices or penny-pinch. Find the best possible cat of your chosen breed, and purchase it. In the long run, a top-quality, healthy purebred cat is always the wisest choice.

***Opposite:** A cat is an independent creature whose need for its own "space" should be respected. Persian.*

## PLACE OF PURCHASE

Cats can be obtained in a variety of ways: pet shops, breeders, humane societies and animal shelters. Each of these establishments has their advantages and with little exception, are pet-quality cats and do not possess "star quality." Ideally, they are healthy and hardy. Store keepers will be fully informed to provide you with the animal's

*With so many lovely breeds from which to choose, deciding on your special cat may not be easy. Manx kittens.*

disadvantages. The advantage of purchasing a cat from a pet shop is that you get what you see. Most pet shops can provide the future owner with a variety of breeds and colors within those breeds. These animals, pedigree, breeder's name and address, as well as the appropriate registration materials. Additionally, information on the cat's inoculations and specifics on health should be accessible from the seller. Customers are always right, at least when asking questions. If your pet-shop keeper cannot answer all your questions about the cat you wish to purchase, go to another source.

Breeders are a second option for the potential cat keeper. Names and addresses of breeders can be located in the classified section of all major fancy publications. Visiting a cat show is another way of acquiring breeder information. The dates of current cat shows are advertised in publications or can be acquired by contacting a major cat registry (e.g., Cat Fanciers' Association or Governing Council of the Cat Fancy). Potential owners are sure to find a visit to a cat show a delightful experience. Not only will you be surrounded by fellow cat lovers, you will meet prominent breeders in the company of their best cats. Seeing 20 to 30 breeds

of cats, in various colors, can also help you to decide which breed of cat you like best. Breeders and other show people love to talk "cats" and will be willing to tell you about the breed, its advantages, and personality pluses. (Some may even

*Before you select your cat, you should consider the amount of time that you can devote to its grooming. Persian kittens.*

it that they are well-adjusted, properly fed, and healthy in every respect. This kind of assurance cannot be attained from any source other than a good breeder.

Animal shelters or welfare organizations are another

*Kittens will literally spend hours together in playful camaraderie.*

*This little tyke's scholarly pose is amusing; however, most cats will not submit to such photographic endeavors.*

point out the breed's lesser points, if asked tactfully.) It is also important that the owner get acquainted with the breeder—you can tell a lot about a breeder's stock and the temperament/sociability of his kittens from the breeder's own personality. The best breeders are responsible in the rearing and socialization of their kittens. These quality cat fanciers are concerned about the cats themselves, seeing to

*The condition of your prospective kitten's health should be your primary consideration. Bicolored shorthair and tabby shorthair.*

possible source to obtain a cat. These establishments occasionally offer a purebred cat for adoption, although their usual offering consists mostly of strayed mixed breeds. More than likely, a cat offered from a shelter will be an adult or adolescent; kittens rarely are seen in shelters. As with pet shops, it is important to make sure that no illness or infection has spread to your potential pet from the animals around it. Additionally such animals can be suffering from stress and fatigue. If acquiring the cat from a rescue mission, shelter or pet shop, the most advisable route is to take the animal to the vet before you go home to have it checked for ailments or conditions.

## THE PICK OF THE LITTER

There are six vital signs which you should check for before purchasing a cat or kitten. The eyes must be clean and bright. A cat's eyes are good indicators of its overall condition. As with all these signs, the vitality and health of the cat can be determined by close examination. Clean ears and

*In spite of the cat's aloofness and apparent self-sufficiency, your love and attention can make of this pet a wonderful lasting friend.*

*Note the luxuriant quality of this Manx's coat. The overall care that a cat receives is reflected in the animal's general appearance. Owner, Raymond R. Freiberger.*

clean nose are the next two signs of good health. Discharge of any kind (from the eyes, ears and nose) suggest less than optimal condition. Check the mouth, pink gums, white, clean teeth—no sign of bad breath. The coat should be resilient and glossy. Traces of fleas or scurf infestation can be checked for. While fleas can be eliminated from the host animal, these parasites are also linked to other maladies. Lastly check that the anal region is clean, not stained or red—no sign of diarrhea or tapeworm infestation.

The abdomen, somewhat flat, should not appear overly round as this may be a sign of roundworms. On males, check that its testicles are intact—fear not when you notice the penis is missing, it is not an external organ in the cat and is located within a small round opening below the anus.

The movement of the cat can also be observed. By age

*This striking feline is a Birman. Its point colors can be seal, chocolate, blue, or lilac—all of which contrast nicely with the pure white "gloves" on the feet. Owner, Betty A. Cowles.*

eight weeks, a kitten has been able to move with coordination for about two weeks so any signs of hobbling or lameness cannot be attributed to the kitten's age. Such a lack of coordination may indicate that the litter is afflicted with panleucopenia or a dietary deficiency.

## MATCHMAKING

As if the fates orchestrate the pairing of felines to their keepers, many fanciers believe that you should choose the cat that appeals to you, and the other details will fall into place. Provided that you know the breeder and respect his method of socialization and rearing, choosing the right individual should be a pleasure. The temperament of purebred cats, despite the guidelines indicated in many breed standards, vary from breed member to breed member. Within a litter of Siamese

*The Russian Blue is renowned for its independent spirit and keen intelligence.*

cats, for instance, a good number of the cats may be outgoing and lively, but others may be shy, aggressive, timid or unruly. Temperaments are nurtured by the queen and fostered by

*The Aby's sweet expression can be attributed to the gentle contours of the cheeks and browline.*

oldest of all cat breeds, with support of this claim coming in the form of ancient Egyptian paintings and sculptures. To this day, however, considerable controversy rages about the true origin of the breed. But this talk of history is not to detract in any way from the Aby breed, which is one of the most intelligent, personable, and loyal of felines. The Abyssinian is a lithe yet muscular cat of action and interest in its surroundings. The head is a modified, slightly rounded wedge without flat planes. The ears are large, alert, and moderately pointed. Most important is the color of the coat. Ruddy, red and blue coat colors are double or triple ticked with distinct, even, and contrasting dark- and light-colored bands. The ruddy brown coat is ticked with various shades of black or dark brown, and is sometimes called burnt-

considered by some to be the ancestor of most domestic cats. The Abyssinian is considered by most cat fanciers to be among the

sienna. The red coat is ticked with chocolate brown, with a deep red undercoat. The blue coat is soft blue-gray, with slate blue ticking in various degrees; undercoat is ivory. In all three colors, the undercoat is clear and bright to the skin. Eyes are gold or green, preference to rich, deep colors. Tail tips are colored darker according to darkest ticking. There also exists a longcoated version of the Abyssinian breed, called the Somali, especially suitable for owners who admire the characteristics of the Aby but who adore the long-coated cat. Somalis are

*Fanciers of the Aby love the breed for its pleasant personality, sense of humor, and love of people. Owner, Dean Mastrangelo.*

*As American as apple pie is the American Shorthair, a sturdy, rugged cat that made his way to the New World along with other early settlers.*

not surprisingly called the British Shorthair, and the domestic shorthairs of France, Germany, and other European countries are collectively called European Shorthairs. Regarding the history of the breed, there is little that can be told, excepting recent events. Essentially, the first American Shorthairs arrived as immigrant British and European Shorthairs with the first of America's settlers. Once in North America, the cats quickly adapted to the rigors of the New World. The first American Shorthairs undoubtedly were farm cats, working cats, large-boned yet agile, fearless yet docile. In the early 1900s breeders began to breed seriously for type and quality. The American Shorthair of today, as recognized as an individual breed, is quite distinct from its farm-cat ancestors and especially from

gaining wide acceptance in the show world and enjoy a strong following.

## American Shorthair

The American Shorthair is America's own version of the classic domestic shorthair found through North America and Europe. Britain too has her own shorthair, the street cats and alley cats of this day. The American Shorthair is a strongly built, well-balanced, symmetrical cat of power, endurance and agility. The head is large, with full cheeks; the eyes are large and wide, with the upper lid shaped like half an almond; the body medium in length and bone; the coat is short, thick, even and hard in texture, with regional difference allowed because of the coat's adapting to climate. Colors form a myriad, with most every possible color of a cat acceptable.

*Intelligent, beautiful, and even-tempered, the American Shorthair can make an excellent companion cat for people of all ages.*

***Above and Opposite:*** *Sometimes referred to as a longhaired Siamese, the Balinese is a not a hybrid, but rather a mutation—and a lovely one at that.*

### Balinese

The Balinese, in all its long-coated beauty, is simply a Siamese with an ermine coat. It is generally accepted that the breed is not the result of outcrossing or hybridization but occurred as a spontaneous mutation within the Siamese breed. This fact is important, for if other breeds were introduced in creation of the Bali, then some of the appealing characteristics could have been lost. Historians assure us that such is not the case: the Balinese is Siamese. Although it is likely that longhaired mutations occurred very early in the Siamese breed, it was not until the 1940s that breeders made serious attempts to further the mutation. The longcoated mutation calls for a long single coat, as opposed to the double coats of many long-coated cats. The ideal Balinese is svelte in appearance, with long tapering lines, is very lithe but strong and muscular. The head is a long tapering wedge. The ears are strikingly large, pointed, and wide at their base. Acceptable colors are identical to those of the Siamese breed, namely seal point, chocolate point, blue point, and lilac point. Blue eyes are an absolute must. In addition to the blue of the eye, owner must check against crossed-eyedness and "quivering" eyes, to which the Siamese breed types have demonstrated a proclivity. The Balinese typically matures more quickly than other longhaired breeds. Outcrosses to the Siamese are still allowed but should be conducted only by knowledgeable, experienced breeders.

## Birman

Know also as the Sacred Cat of Burma, the Birman breed is believed to have

*The Birman's appearance is deceivingly delicate: beneath the regal flowing coat is a sturdy feline of remarkable prowess and agility.*

originated in Burma, where they served as companions and spiritual guardians of Temple priests. The first members of the breed to leave their native country reportedly entered France as a pair around the year 1919. The male reportedly succumbed to illness shortly after arriving, but fortunately for the breed in the Western world, the female was pregnant from the male. From this very limited breed base, it is believed that the breed as we know it today came to be. The Birman is a large, stocky cat, with long silky hair that is not given to matting, which is fortunate for groomers. The coat forms a heavy ruff around the neck and is slightly curly on the stomach. Color may be seal point, blue point, lilac point, or chocolate point; desirable in all point colors is the "golden mist," which is a faint golden beige cast on the

*The Birman's fur is not subject to mats or tangles; thus, Birmans require less grooming than other longhaired cat breeds.*

back and sides. Distinctive to the breed are its gloves: each of the four feet must be colored pure white. The eyes are almost round, and always blue in color—the deeper the blue the better. There also exists a short-coated Birman, which is called the Snowshoe, but the breed is not commonly recognized by major registries. The Birman is generally a quiet and affectionate feline, although given to sudden bursts of energy. These are surprisingly agile and athletic cats despite their elegant appearance.

***Above and Opposite:*** *The color and sheen of the Bombay's coat immediately capture the viewer's attention, while the copper-colored eyes set against the black coat make for a striking contrast.*

### Bombay

The pantherlike Bombay was developed from black American Shorthairs and a sable Burmese. The result is a dashing black cat with a satinlike coat. The look of the Bombay evokes ecstatic responses from new fanciers, who concur that the Bombay is distinctive and exquisite. The Bombay's head, without flat planes, is very round with chubby cheeks. A

short, strong muzzle with a visible break. Considerable breadth between the eyes and tapering. Eyes, round in shape, and ears, tilting forward and broad, are both set far apart. The body does not appear rangy, and is always perfectly proportioned. The coat is truly satiny in texture with a sheen that appears almost artificial, although it is very real. The black coat, black

*The Bombay exhibits the black color and hardy type of the black American Shorthair and the satin-like coat of the Burmese.*

*Besides its good looks, the Bombay is loved for its even temperament and playful personality.*

like an Indian panther, is enhanced by the breed's copper eyes. Color is the most important feature of the Bombay breed. The breed was created in the late 1950s in the American South. Disregarding the coat, the Bombay would appear as little more than a Burmese. These are truly remarkable cats that love the indoors. Little grooming is required, though much play and attention is. They are curious and energetic—a favorite of children. The personality of the Bombay varies tremendously, perhaps more so than with other breeds. Some attribute this to the varied beginnings of these cats, and admittedly American Shorthairs, used to create the breed, have dazzlingly different temperaments and proclivities. Others simply believe that the Bombay is such an individualist that it refuses to conform to a standard character. They do concur with the standard on color however.

*The British Shorthair, sizeable and strong, is Britain's counterpart to the American Shorthair. This robust chap is noted for his charming ways and laid-back approach to life.*

### British Shorthair

American readers may view the British Shorthair as an elite British breed, whereas in truth the breed derives from street cats that wandered about the homes, pubs, and neighborhoods of jolly ole England. These are rugged, hardy felines, much the equivalent to the U.S.'s American Shorthair, or even Europe's European Shorthair. Essentially all these breeds are street cats with a show world fancy. In appearance, the British Shorthair is a well-balanced, unexaggerated cat. The head is round and massive in structure; the forehead, too, should be rounded with a flattish plane on the top of the skull. The eyes are alert, large, and round. The British Shorthair is no small cat; it is well-knit and powerful—medium to large in size. A level back and deep, broad chest modify the cat's power, as do the sturdy legs. The coat is very easy care, and resistant to the weather. It is short and very dense with much body. Colors vary as they do for other domestic shorthairs. Among the registries' accepted colors are: red, white, blue, black, cream, chinchilla, smokes, tabbies, patches, and bi-colors. British Shorthairs make good pets as they have been survivors and people-cats for many generations. They are obedient and naturally bright. Their mousing instincts are largely intact making this level-headed feline a super work cat too.

**Burmese**

The choice of many cat lovers requiring a distinctive cat, the Burmese is a medium-sized, somewhat compact cat with a flawless head. Owners accredit the Burmese with limitless

*Burmese kittens. Members of this attractive breed are medium-sized, with good bone structure and musculature.*

entertainment abilities, as clowns and vaudevillians; other fanciers acclaim the cat for its vocal abilities—they are surely boisterous and always have a lot to say. The fullness or robustness of the cat varies from the United States to Great Britain; in the latter a more foreign body type is preferred. The Burmese has a glossy, fine and satinlike coat which is short and close-lying. This glossiness is very important to selecting the right cat—a quality adult Burmese has a sheen which reflects proper breeding and feeding. Cats occurred originally in sable brown, reportedly from a Siamese mutation. Today in the U.S., champagne, described as a warm honey beige, shading toward a light goldish tan; blue, a medium tone with warm fawn undertones; and platinum, a silvery gray with pale fawn undertones also occur.

In England, red, brown tortie, cream, blue tortie, chocolate tortie, and lilac tortie also color the Burmese. The Burmese is a hardy, long-lived cat that

***Below and Opposite:** If you desire a pet that is affectionate and sociable—a real "people"cat—the Burmese is the cat for you.*

*The short coat of the Burmese is shiny and thick.*

appreciates human attention. Most cats are very intelligent and can be taught to do tricks that most others would scarcely attempt. For the owner who demands a lead-trained cat, the Burmese is a great prospect since it is short coated and highly amenable to lead training. Additionally, the short coat requires a minimum of grooming, although a good once–over the coat will help to keep the natural sheen of the fur. The breed, apparently bred for good looks as well as outgoing personality, are described as soulful and unreserved, making them wonderful cats to own and love.

**Chartreux**

The Chartreux, also known as the British Blue, is a relative newcomer to the world of purebred cats. This sturdy French breed first peered its head at American cat shows in 1986, and has been turning heads since. Chartreux are prized for their mousing abilities for the robustness and vigor of the breed are proverbial. Familiar with proverbs, too, the Chartreux boasts a romantic history connecting

*Of French origin is the Chartreux, an amiable and amenable feline that can be doggedly devoted to its master.*

it to favoring monks who carried the cats back to France from South Africa. In the monasteries, the cats were highly regarded though not spoiled, since today this breed continues to be a working cat. Careful selection guarantees the potential Chartreux owner a cat very strong and nearly doglike in its devotion to its master. The body of the Chartreux is athletic, well developed; the shoulders are broad, the chest deep. Bone and muscle are solid and comparatively massive. Either you like blue cats or you don't! If you do,

consider the Chartreux which comes in many shades of blue-gray from dark to light, ash to slate. The somewhat woolly coat, colored in blue-gray, is an important feature of the breed. The eyes are a golden copper and the paw pads are rose-taupe. Chartreux kittens are precocious, not reaching adulthood until three years of age. At four months, the kittens are ready for their new homes. This is a good-natured and pleasant cat that does not impose upon its owner. Caring for a Chartreux is simple and rewarding.

*Left and Opposite:*
*Chartreux are easy to keep and a pleasure to own.*

*If you want a cat with the talents and abilities of a Siamese, but one that offers different color varieties, consider the Colorpoint Shorthair.*

### Colorpoint Shorthair

The Colorpoint Shorthair is a beautiful breed of smooth-coated cat that, for no small reason, resembles the celebrated Siamese breed. The cats were derived from Siamese breedings. Dilute mutations in the Siamese procured these colorpointed felines. Siamese breed purists were outraged and did not fancy these chocolate-, blue-, and lilac-pointed cats to be registered as Siamese. Persons who favored the new color scheme on the mutated Siamese secured the breed the U.S. today recognizes as a Colorpoint Shorthair. It follows then that the care for a Colorpoint is similar to caring for a Siamese, since they are quite the same cat. Abyssinian crosses were also involved so the temperament of the Colorpoint is somewhat different than that of the Siamese. In body type, the Colorpoint breed is medium in size—the body is beautifully balanced, with a pleasing combination of the fine bone and good musculature. The tail is long, thin, and tapering to a point. The coat is fine textured like the Siamese's. Colors include: red, cream, seal-lynx, chocolate-lynx, lilac-lynx, red-lynx, seal-tortie, chocolate-tortie, blue-cream, lilac-cream, seal tortie-lynx, chocolate tortie-lynx, blue-cream lynx, lilac-cream lynx, and cream lynx. Eye color is invariably a deep vivid blue. From all these wonderful colors, the new owner can choose the shade of cat which best agrees with his palate. Fanciers bored of

the Siamese can jazz up their favorite cat by considering a Colorpoint Shorthair. Like the ever-popular, though less colorful Siamese, this cat is affectionate, inquisitive, smart and very vocal.

**Cornish Rex**

Described as a curvilinear cat, the Cornish Rex is unique for many reasons. Quite obviously, this is not just an ordinary cat and no

*Cornish Rex. This breed—born of normally coated parents—caused quite a sensation when it first appeared in Cornwall, England.*

*The Cornish Rex's appearance is the result of a mutation that reduces guard hairs and produces a wavy coat.*

Cornish Rex owner need contend with his cat being mistaken for a street cat. The Rex's most apparently unique feature is its extremely soft and wavy coat, a coat that is curly, curly, curly, and silky too. The whiskers too are curly! The coat lies close to the body, with wave extending from the top of the head to the tail tip. The gentle curves of the Rex and its petite, delicate appearance should not mislead the potential owner. The Cornish Rex is a sturdy cat with a solid frame and impressive musculature. Although too smart to attempt to outrun a Greyhound, the Rex has been compared to that two-story sighthound on more than one occasion. These are people-oriented cats who get bored relatively quickly. The Rex personality is tremendous, always active in body and mind. Owners rarely need to guess their Rex's intentions, since these cats are very expressive creatures, capable of sharing even the most subtle of observations. Another adjective which has been attached to the Rex is "hypoallergenic", meaning that the cat is recommended for cat admirers who have sworn off felines because of allergies. In color the Rex can be a variety of colors including solids, tabbies, tortoise shell, calicos, creams, and bi-colors.

## Cymric

The Cymric, pronounced *kim-rick*, is a longhaired spin–off of the Manx. It is one of the few breeds of cat that is tailless. Of course the Manx is another. This breed is a natural mutation of the Manx and is not a result of crossbreeding in a different breed of cat. Its general appearance, except its coat, is that of the Manx, and its temperament and personality are nearly identical. These are sturdy and adaptable cats with much heart and pride.

*The Cymric, a longhaired version of the Manx (a tailless breed), is one of the newer breeds of cat that is gaining popularity in the cat fancy.*

Since Manx die-hards were not enamored of the prospect of a mutant Manx, the breed opted for the name Cymric. These wonderful Welsh cats are deserving of such a name since only cats from the Isle of Man were involved in the creation of the longhaired variety. The coat in question is double; medium in length,

*Above: The Cymric is known for his pleasant temperament and loveable personality. Owner, Margaret Rickard. **Opposite:** Red and white Cymric owned by Vickie Hansen.*

with gradual increase in length from shoulders to rump. Breeches, abdomen, and neck ruff to be longer

*The Devon Rex is a highly individualistic breed of cat that exhibits a keen interest in the world around him.*

than rest of body coat, though coat is generally long all over; lower leg and head coat to be shorter. Tufts to the toes and ears are preferred.

### Devon Rex

The Devon Rex defies most of our notions as to what a cat should look like and since cats most unanimously despise preconceptions, expectations, and restrictions, the Devon Rex is able to capitalize on uniqueness and the unexpected. The most obvious feature of the Rex cats is the coat. The density, texture, length, and waviness of the Devon's coat are all especially prized. Like the Cornish, the Devon has a rippling coat, particularly on the areas where the coat is the densest—the back, sides, legs, tail, face, and ears; overall the cat is well covered with fur. Exaggerated baldness disqualifies a cat from competition. The Devon's body is long and muscular, quite Oriental. The legs are sturdy, carrying the body high; hind legs somewhat longer than forelegs. Tail, very long and tapering, covered with fine short fur. Colors vary tremendously. Solids in white, black, blue, red, cream, chocolate, cinnamon, lavender, and fawn; in most solids the eyes are gold. Bi-colors, tabbies, and mottled colorations occur. The Devon Rex is an affectionate, active cat who is surprisingly solid when picked up. Like its Cornish cousin, the Devon looks far more fragile than it is in reality. The Devon is not to be confused with any elegant breed of cat; they are impulsive and unpredictable. While enjoying human attention, Devons don't sit pretty for company. Owners describe these cats as food bandits and trotters, as well as retrievers and talkers. A quiet, ornamentlike cat to dress up the condo is not the Devon and such owners are advised to search elsewhere, perhaps a ceramic shoppe.

**Egyptian Mau**

The Egyptian Mau is a lithe spotted cat of very speckled origins. Some fanciers acclaim the Mau as the only natural breed of spotted cat, one in the same with the cats appearing on the walls of the Temple at

*The lustrous spotted coat of the Egyptian Mau contributes to the breed's visual appeal.*

*Fanciers of the breed maintain that the Mau can make a very loving and devoted pet.*

Shebese (circa 1400 B.C.). Joyful babble still foams about "Baba" and "Jojo" from Cairo lines imported to Italy. Whatever the beginnings of the Mau, it stands out as a very special, gifted breed of cat which has been known in the States since the 1950s. Today the breed is widely accepted in America and Europe. In intelligence and demeanor, the Mau is a prize of a cat. Loyalty and devotion to its own are second nature to the Egyptian Mau, who never shuns human attention when offered. Its needs are few, and grooming its fine and silky coat is no chore. Brushing to enhance the lustrous sheen of the breed helps to keep the coat resilient and clean. Spotted cats have become more and more in vogue and the Egyptian Mau is one of the first of such felines to show its true spotted colors, which include incidentally: silver, bronze, smoke, and pewter.

While less common, cinnamon, blue, and lilac are presently being promoted. The gooseberry green eyes of the Mau make this cat more irresistible than other spotted felines, some confess. The Mau pattern requires clear contrast between the ground and markings. Foreheads are emblazoned by clearly perceptible "M" and frown marks; a dorsal stripe, heavily banded tail, mascara-marked cheeks, and an underbelly "Vest Button" are characteristically celebrated. In body type, the Mau is moderately long, with definite musculation and balance. Legs are proportionate to the body; the hind longer than the fore. Feet are small, nearly round. Thick at the base, the tail is medium length, slightly tapering.

*Exotic Shorthair. Exotics are alert, intelligent cats with outgoing personalities.*

whiskers be of the same uniform coloration. The head of the Havana is longer than wide, the head forms essentially a wedge, which is more apparent in British–born cats than in American Havanas. The breed is medium in length, very firm and muscular. Males tend to be larger than females, though both sexes are perfectly balanced. The cat's body structure is mid-range between cobby and svelte. While Havanas enjoy human company, they have a natural propensity for self-entertainment and are never (hardly ever) destructive. These Cuban migrants are somehow more nosy than other cats and can be very insistent upon attention. To groom a Havana, a weekly once-over the coat with a double-sided rubber brush and a chamois will keep the coat resilient and glossy. As the cat grows older, its coat color will darken. An adult Havana weighs six to ten pounds. Show cats must be solid colored without any shading; even the whiskers must be brown.

*The pairing of a Siamese and a Persian produced this beauty: the Himalayan. Elegant and intelligent, the Himmy is cherished by many in the cat fancy.*

### Himalayan

The Himalayan, known as the Colourpoint Longhair in Great Britain and also as the Colorpoint Persian, enjoys great world-wide popularity as a breed with the beauty of

*The Himalayan is so named because of its similarity in coloration to that of the Himalayan rabbit.*

coat characteristic of the Persian and the beauty of markings characteristic of the Siamese. An additional outstanding feature of the pointed Himalayan is its blue eyes, which are large, round, and full. Breeding and showing Himalayans can be a tricky matter to the novice, but experienced persons typically have little trouble discerning the nuances. Himalayans, though a pure-breed, are still crossed back to Persians, and non-pointed Himalayan offspring (though not exhibiting the called-for points of the breed standard) are eligible for championship competition under some show-governing bodies. Besides showing and breeding considerations, the Himalayan's grooming requisites need to be accounted for by the potential owner. Himalayans, with their long, silky coats that measure over 4½ inches in length, require meticulous daily grooming to keep their coats from matting and snarling. Characteristic coat details include a neck ruff which continues to between the front legs, forming a frill; a full brush tail, and long ear and toe tufts. Acceptable colorpoints for the Himalayan breed include: seal, chocolate, blue, lilac, flame, tortie, and blue-cream; other colors include chocolate solid and lilac solid. Eyes of pointed cats

*Sporting but a stub of a tail, the Japanese Bobtail is a most distinguishable cat. Japanese Bobtails are extroverts that enjoy being with people.*

*Good looks and a pleasant personality lend to the appeal of the Japanese Bobtail.*

almost invariably a deep, vivid blue, while those of the solid colored cats typically a brilliant copper.

## Japanese Bobtail

As told in its name, the Japanese Bobtail is a short-tailed breed of cat. Breed experts believe that each tail is unique, and that no one member of the breed has yet to possess the perfect pom-pom, which many breeders strive to produce. Indeed, there is considerable variance to the short-tailed feature of the breed, and some specimens have exhibited tails five inches long, and some longer; but such lengths are generally not allowed in the show ring. Besides the breed's featured tail, though distinguishing, the personality of the

*Despite his self-reliant nature, the Japanese Bobtail has the capacity to be quite affectionate with his human family.*

Japanese Bobtail is pointed out by most fanciers as being an endearing characteristic of the breed: the Japanese Bobtail is known as a breed with personality. This feature is not surprising in a breed which has been keenly domesticated for centuries, and the Japanese Bobtail believably traces back at least 1,000 years. The Bobtail is generally extroverted and likes to share both its play and its quiet times with humans. The traditional color of the breed, which is also the most popular, casts large, distinct black and red patches on a background white base, which is called Mi-Ke (mee-kay) in the breed's native Japan. Other recognized colors include: white, black and red; bicolors of black and white, and red and white; tricolor and tortoiseshell (black, red, and cream). Odd eyes occur and are considered most attractive with the traditional color pattern. Despite the breed's ornate appearance, these are no pillow pussies: as hardy as they are energetic, Japanese Bobtails display a centuries-old resume of ratting and mousing in their native land, where they were protectors of the silk trade, and guardians of the rice fields. The breed is short coated and thus requires little grooming time.

**Javanese**

The Javanese is one of several Siamese variants, and thus it displays many of the

*Javanese. The influence of the Siamese on this breed is readily apparent in the lithe body conformation.*

characteristics of its renowned mother breed. More directly, however, the Javanese descends from the Balinese, which is a longhaired mutation of the Siamese. In essence, the Javanese is a Balinese in other than the four recognized Balinese colors (Seal Point, Blue Point, Chocolate Point, and Lilac Point). The Javanese can exhibit all the same colors as the Colorpoint Shorthair, and thus can display 16 coat colors, either pointed or lynx-pointed. Other than color, the Javanese is physically very similar to the Balinese—fine, lithe, and definitely oriental. The ears are notably large, wide at the base and pointed at the tip, and the eyes show the classic Siamese almond shape, slanting harmoniously towards the nose. Like the other Siamese-type breeds, the Javanese is slightly given to crossed eyes and "quivering" eyes. These traits, though usually harmless physically, are

**Opposite and Above:** *The Javanese offers all the beautiful color possibilities of the Colorpoint Shorthair.*

undesirable in all Siamese-type breeds, and potential owners are encouraged to check the eyes before purchase, while potential breeders are asked not to breed Javanese displaying these traits.

*Above:* The Korat is an intelligent, ever curious feline that can make a devoted pet. *Opposite:* Large luminous eyes are hallmarks of the breed.

### Korat

The Korat exhibits a striking appearance brought about by its distinctive heart-shaped head, characteristically green eyes, and unshaded silver-tipped silver-blue coat. Adding appeal to this attractive cat is its long history, as many histories assert that the Korat is among the first cats mentioned in written history. The Korat believably originated in the Korat province (after which it is, of course, named) of Thailand, where the breed was called *Si-Sawat* and was revered as a good-luck charm. The breed first reached the United States in 1959, Europe in 1972, and breeders throughout the

world have worked hard to preserve the breed's type as evidenced throughout history. Although many cat lovers trace the Korat to Siam (called Thailand until 1939), the breed does not exhibit the classic Siamese type. Obviously, however, the Korat in no way suggests a Siamese, and meticulous breeding practices through the many centuries of the breed is the oft-offered reason for this. The Korat is a muscular and round cat, well proportioned; its ears are large and set high; its coat is described as short to medium in length, glossy and fine, lying close to the body. Essentially the breed is an easycare animal, with grooming, feeding, and exercise requirements those of the typical hardy cat. Experienced owners cite that the breed prefers quiet homes but bask in affection and delight with their intelligence. Ironically, the breed faces danger of extinction in its native land, which suffered greatly during the past Asian wars. This decimation resulted in a limited breed base from which foreign (American and European) breeders could construct their own breeding programs. Through diligence

*The Korat is happiest in a calm, relaxed home environment.*

*The Maine Coon, bright, handsome, and sturdy, is noted for his extraordinary mousing abilities.*

and hard work, they succeeded, and the Korat today, though still not of great number, enjoys a strong world-wide following.

## Maine Coon Cat

The heavy, shaggy coat stands as a hallmark of this hardy American breed. Creatively considered a "native" American, though felines are not indigenous to North America, Maine Coons have existed and prospered in the north east United States at least since colonial times. One ambitious theory regarding their origin claims that Vikings brought with them working cats to control sea-

*Its heavy, abundant coat enables the Maine Coon to withstand the rigors of a cold climate.*

faring vermin on their trans-Atlantic voyage(s), and that these cats, left behind in the wilds of the New World, formed the base for today's Maine Coon Breed. A more widely accepted claim for the inception of the breed crosses domestic American shorthairs with Angoras. In either case the Maine Coon was, and still is, a solid, strong, rugged breed, adorned with a smooth, shaggy coat, and able to withstand harsh climates.

For many years, the breed was left to fend for itself in northeast America, and fanciers claim that those times allowed for a natural selection process which gives the breed its hardy constitution today. The Maine Coon is a muscular, broad-chested cat, with a medium-length, medium-width skull; large, well-tufted ears; and large, expressive, well-set eyes. Other than the daily grooming required of the coat, the Maine Coon provides many years of undemanding feline companionship. The breed comes in over twenty coat colors, which can be categorized into five classes: solids, tabby, tabby with whites, partis, and smokes.

**Malayan**

The Malayan is essentially a color variant of the Burmese breed, and it is recognized as a separate breed only in the United States, and then only by some registries. When the Burmese was first accepted

*For all-around adaptability, the Maine Coon is hard to beat. Members of this breed are intelligent, friendly cats who will delight you with their amusing and affectionate ways.*

*Adult Malayan and kittens. The Malayan is a look-alike of the Burmese, from which it differs only in color.*

as a breed, it was considered essential that members of the breed be a warm, solid brown. However, after years of breeding, such colors as champagne, blue, platinum, and fawn began to occur with predictable regularity, and fanciers of these alternative colors wished to register them. Many registries agreed that these colors should be registered and adapted their Burmese standards to include the alternative colors. Other registries adhered to the concept of the Burmese as a sable brown cat. Owners who wish to show their Malayan, or their other-than-sable Burmese, are encouraged to find out the registration and championship policies of their chosen registry. Except for color, the Malayan is essentially a Burmese, both physically and temperamentally. The body is medium in size, muscular and compact. The head is visibly rounded and without flat planes. The coat is glossy, fine and satinlike; it is close-lying and resilient.

## Manx

A Manx cat ideally has no trace of a tail, with a decided hollow at the end of the backbone where in a different breed the tail would begin. The tailless trait is the result of the mutation, and exactly how and when the mutation first occurred remains a mystery, a topic of debate, and the subject of many a tale. One legend tells of Samson's cutting off the tail of the cat in penalty of its entangling him during his swim past the Isle of Man.

*Charming legends abound regarding how this cat, the Manx, "lost" its tail; in actuality, its taillessness is the result of a mutation.*

Another legend reports a tailless cat left by the Spanish Armada, which arrived at the Isle in 1588. And perhaps the most oft-cited legend accuses Noah with haste, claiming that he, in his hurry to batten down against the rains, slammed the door to the Ark on a pair of cats, thus creating a tailless breed. Today's consensus holds that the Manx breed originated many centuries ago on the Isle of Man, off the coast of Great Britain, but how exactly the breed, or the cats which fathered the breed, arrived at the island remains unknown. The first impression of the Manx, besides its taillessness, is that of roundness; the head is round, with a firm round muzzle and prominent cheeks; the chest is broad, positioned on short, substantial front legs; the short back arches from the shoulders to a round rump;

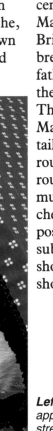

*Left and Opposite:* The general appearance of the Manx is one of strength and power. The body is solid, compact, and of great depth.

JALDuncan

***Above:*** *The overall roundness of the Manx's rump is a characteristic of the breed.* ***Opposite:*** *An odd-eyed Manx.*

there is a great depth of flank; the thighs are muscular and, of course, rounded. In ideal specimens there is no trace of a tail. However, a rise of the bones at the end of the spine is allowed and not penalized in most show circles unless it is severe (often considered such when it stops the judge's hand when passing over the area). The coat of the Manx is double, short and dense, with a well-padded quality due to the longer, open outer coat and the close, cottony undercoat. The Manx sports many possible colors, including white, black, blue, red, chinchilla, blue smoke, silver patched tabby, cream tabby, calico and tortoiseshell.

## Norwegian Forest

A true outdoors cat, the Norwegian Forest Cat or Norsk Skaukatt is the people's cat of Norway. In that country, the cat has been recognized as a breed unto itself since the 1930s. As a hunter, this cat is superior, rivaling the American Shorthair as a mouser. It is a large breed of domestic cat which resembles the Maine Coon of the United States. Had these two cats lived in the same country, they would have undoubtedly melded together into one very big and robust outdoor feline. The tail of the Norwegian Forest cat resembles that of a raccoon, were there coons in Norway for it to mimic. The forests of Norway have spun more than its share of myths

*Below:* The Norwegian Forest Cat is a rugged individual with a fierce sense of independence. *Opposite:* Members of the breed sport an abundant ruff.

*The Norwegian Forest Cat's lush coat requires regular grooming to keep it looking its best.*

chested conformation of the cat is impressive. The legs are firmly boned; the paws large and round. The coat of the cat must be groomed regularly; it is thick and double, provides the cat with protection from harsh Norwegian climes. Cats come in a variety of colors and have never been bred specifically for color; hardiness and health were essential to survival of these cats. Few cats are found outside of Norway today.

and legends and the cat from that forest hasn't been excluded from such fables. The enchanted abilities and strength of the Norwegian Forest Cat have been well-recognized and recorded by the Norwegian people. The head is round and notably large. The muscular, broad-

### Ocicat

A new hybrid on the block, the spotted Ocicat was derived from crosses of certain shorthaired breeds to attain the desired look. That desired look is one of an untamed agouti–spotted cat bred selectively to emulate

***Opposite:** The Ocicat's distinctive look can be traced to its Abyssinian and Siamese heritage.*

the wild cats. Like the California Spangled, the Ocicat is meant to distract humans' minds from poaching the great cats of the wild as well as to sway them from wanting to keep smaller domestic with little needs out of the ordinary. These are outgoing, playful cats with little reservations. Smart and biddable, the Ocicat is winning friends in cat circles with natural ease.

*Ocicats are energetic, active cats who take a keen interest in the goings-on around them.*

ones as pets. Ocelots and margays at one time were becoming popular as pets. The Ocicat is a true "exotic" cat that is 100 percent The colors which the breed offers include: silver, chocolate, cinnamon, blue, lavender, fawn, tawny, chocolate, and lilac. Eye

*The Oriental Shorthair—sometimes described as a solid-colored Siamese—is a svelte and lithe cat with long, tapering lines.*

color can be any color other than blue; deep colors preferred. The distinctive patterns of the Ocicat of course turn the most heads. The face is colored lighter than the rest of the body; the tail tip, the darkest. In build, the Ocicat is athletic and sinewy, projecting a refined and controlled image.

**Oriental Shorthair**

The Oriental Shorthair (sometimes called Foreign) is a colorful breed of Siamese type. Ranging far beyond the four accepted colors of the Siamese breed, the Oriental Shorthair can be solid, shaded or tortoiseshell, as well as smoke and tabby. The solids include blue,

***Above:*** *Oriental Shorthairs are playful felines with a sparkling personality like that of the Siamese.* ***Opposite:*** *Orientals offer a wide variety of coat colors.*

chestnut, cinnamon, cream, ebony, fawn, lavender, red, and white (as well as caramel in the U.K.)These are called selfs. Eye color is commonly green; white cats may have either blue or green eyes; odd eyes never acceptable. The Oriental Shorthair is considered a breed which brings its owner good luck, a chore which many Oriental domestics have taken upon themselves, since the breed was serendipitously (or accidentally) happened upon by the creators of the Havana Brown. Anatomically speaking, the Oriental adheres to the Siamese body type. The Oriental's many colored coats are deserving of royal attention and fawning. The breed has been described as natty and dashing as well as extreme. These are sensitive and chic felines with wondrously svelte conformations. Tubular well outlines the long, muscular torso of the Oriental. The tail, which is thin at its base, is also lengthy, and tapers to a defined point. Like the Siamese and Havana, the Oriental's coat is close lying, short and fine in texture. In appearance, the coat should be glossy. For those who like the look of the Oriental

Shorthair but prefer longer fur, a longhaired variety also exists and is called, surprisingly enough, the Oriental Longhair.

*Persian kitten. These lovely creatures are the ultimate longhaired breed of cat.*

## Persian

The Persian is known in Great Britain as the Longhair, probably because it is singular in its exuberantly long coat. The Persian coat is virtually the standard by which fanciers compare other longhaired breeds. Long and thick and flowing describe this very full coat. In addition to the undercoat's being woolly and dense, the coat is spectacular for its full brush and extensive ear and toe tufts. The entire body, including the shoulders, is covered by long fur, forming an immense ruff around the neck and filling out the chest and forelegs. The Persian's head is imposing, broad and round; bone structure and face is perfectly round. The

*Opposite: The Persian's luminous, expressive eyes are a trademark of the breed.*

through the course of her pregnancy and maternity. Do not overfeed a Persian, though don't call your plushly coated cat "fatty" too quickly; such a full coat can be very deceptive.

## Russian Blue

The Russian Blue is certainly blue, though the Russian part has been long debated. The thickness and plushness of the cat's coat (it is not long) would indicate that this is a nordic breed of cat. The cat's coat is comparable to the coat of the Siberian Husky or Eskimo Dog in its protective abilities. Other sources expound upon the Russian Blue's eye ridges, said to keep the snow out of the cat's eyes on blizzardy Siberia nights. The author doesn't second such a snow job! Nevertheless, the

*Below:* A unique and eye-catching Russian Blue. **Opposite:** *Tranquil and serene, this breed appreciates a quiet home environment.*

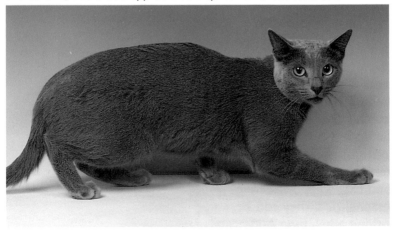

*This cat, the Scottish Fold, often evokes a smile of amusement, due to its curiously folded ears.*

Russian Blue is a hardy blue cat that has been known in the U.S. and England for most of the twentieth century. After difficult times in England associated with the Great War, the breed survives and has become one of the world's well-known pedigreed cats. The body of the Russian Blue is graceful and lithe, despite its impressive substance. These are smart, difficult–to–fool cats that enjoy regular attention from their owners, though they are largely self-reliant. Apartment dwellers need take advantage of these clean, very predictable companion animals. The coat is dense, silky and resilient; it is quite short and fine and colored in an even bright blue throughout, with lighter shades generally preferred. The guard hairs are distinctly tipped in silver giving the cat its sheen.

## Scottish Fold

This kilt-wearing cat derives from the farm cats of Perthshire, Scotland, mutants in litters from the early 1960s. These "mutants" had a curious flopped ear, giving the cats a wonderful, jesterlike look and a mesmerizing gift and the natural timing for comedy. Seriously, the Scottish Fold has two of the most unusual ears in catdom. The standard for the breed describes them as folding forward and downward. Small, the smaller the better, tightly folded ear preferred over a loose fold and large ear. The ears should be set in a caplike fashion to expose a rounded cranium. Ear tips to be rounded. The Scottish Fold is a shorthaired

*Folds are gentle, loveable cats with a natural talent for winning the affections of family and friends.*

cat, although a longhair variety has been supported recently. It is known as the Longhair Scottish Fold. The character traits of the Scottish Fold are similar to the Shorthairs of Britain, that is to say, charming and hardy. Folds are not overpopulous and the owner may have to wait to acquire

*A Siamese, perhaps one of the best known (and most loved) breeds of cat.*

one; not all kittens of Fold lineage will inherit the proper folding ears. In addition to the Scottish Fold's being cuter than a button, they love people and have adapted gloriously to indoor life. This medium sized cat also comes in a variety of colors including: blue, red, white, black, cream, chinchilla, smokes, tabbies, patches, and bi-colors. These lovable and loving cats are ideal for countryfolk who wish to withdraw their mice's visitation rights. Scottish Folds, whether short coated or long coated, make delightful and affectionate pets. Of course the Longhair Scottish Fold is more difficult to acquire than the traditional Fold and requires a bit more grooming time.

**Siamese**

One of the most familiar of all purebred cats, the Siamese is distinctive for its

*Its striking blue eyes are one of the Siamese's most outstanding features.*

long, svelte, and graceful body, its penetratingly beautiful blue eyes and its super-affectionate personality, which it vocalizes well. The head is wedge shaped, long and tapering and medium in size. Ears must be set well apart, large, wide at their base, tapering to a pointed tip; the ears are to continue the lines of the wedge. Eyes are almond-shaped, slanting towards the nose. The body is medium sized and tubular. The Siamese coat is short and fine, with an illustrious luster.

Four colors, complete with

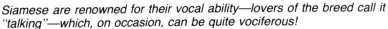

*Siamese are renowned for their vocal ability—lovers of the breed call it "talking"—which, on occasion, can be quite vociferous!*

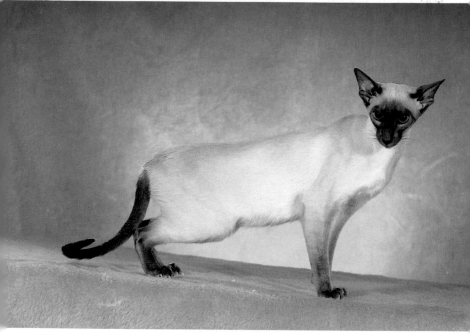

*These extraordinary creatures offer the potential cat owner a loving and remarkably devoted companionship.*

points, are recognized; in the U.K., eight additional colors occur. Unless you are planning to show or breed your purebred Siamese, there is little need to concern yourself with the colorless politics of Siamese cat colors.

For general information purposes, the four Siamese colors in the U.S. are: seal point (pale fawn to cream, shading to underparts, with deep seal brown); chocolate point (unshaded ivory, with milk chocolate); blue point

*A Siamese is an adaptable cat who can be content in just about any environment.*

colored and coated breeds as the Oriental Shorthair, Himalayan, Colorpoint Shorthair, Balinese and Javanese are spin-offs of the Siamese. Siamese cats have a deep devotion to humankind and a true understanding of the human spirit, making them flawless companion animals for the right humans. Their history is closely tied to human spirituality and in Siam (now Thailand) these cats were revered and treasured as companions by society's royalty. Today the Siamese cuddles with the rich and poor alike, though the price of a good Siamese may preclude the latter group. In choosing a Siamese, be very careful to research your source. Type has changed dramatically in the past decades and many of the "high-quality" lines which flaunt apple heads, crossed eyes and kinked tails are deemed today as seriously

(bluish white, shading to white underparts, with deep blue); lilac point (unshaded glacial white, with frosty grey of pinkish tone). The Siamese is an archetype breed and the center of the foreign circle. Such multi-

flawed. These cats will not fend well in the show ring, though they will still make fine companions.

## Singapura

Native of Singapore, the Singapura is a friendly ex-street-dwelling feline which entered the United States in the late 1980s, when it received recognition from both TICA and CFA, the two major cat-registering bodies in the country. It is accepted only in one color, described as sepia—an ivory ground color, ticked with dark brown. The Singapora's head is round, tapering at the outer eye to the definite whisker break, with a broad muzzle. The nose is blunt, with a straight line formed from it to the chin. Ears are large, wide at their base, set at a medium distance on the skull. Eyes are large and almond shaped. Overall this is a small to medium sized feline, with good muscle and bone development. Body length and shoulder height equal in distance. The breed's short coat requires little grooming. These are

*This relative newcomer on the cat scene is the Singapura, who, in years past, went virtually unnoticed as it prowled Singapore streets.*

self-grooming, very clean animals with excellent people-oriented dispositions. The Singapora's curiosity is proverbial and kittens especially need extensive supervision.

**Sphynx**

The Sphynx, hands down, is the most unusual feline in the cat world. This domestic cat is 99 $^{44}/_{100}$% naked! The hairless Sphynx actually carries the genes for

*A Sphynx. Just as one shouldn't judge a book by its cover, one shouldn't judge a cat by its coat—or lack thereof!*

*Even though the Sphynx requires no brushing, he does require regular attention to his skin to keep it soft and supple.*

hairlessness, and it is the only cat that does. These cats occurred in Canadian litters during the mid-1960s (a period known for its favoritism of nudist camps and colonies). Much effort has gone into the breeding and perfecting of the Sphynx type. Early representatives of the breed were little short of pathetic, while today's show-quality cats are admittedly handsome. The hairless mutation does alter the body type, which is essentially foreign, and the breed is genetically more unstable than other established cat breeds. Persons who wish to become associated with the Sphynx as owners or breeders are required to know all the hairy details

involved with these no-hair creatures. Despite its grotesque (or at least unconventional) appearance, the Sphynx is 100% C-A-T. Those who know the Sphynx describe it as a confident, straightforward feline (it has nothing to hide, literally). Advantages and disadvantages abound: for hyperallergic persons, a hairless cat is a dream. The cat's skin, which comes in any color, requires attention. Because of the cat's lack of protection, it can catch colds easily as well as injure itself on sharp objects. These are strictly indoor cats requiring attentive parents, but who would consider letting a naked child out of doors?

**Opposite:** *The crossbreeding of a Siamese and a Burmese yielded this handsome cat: the Tonkinese.*

### Tonkinese

A pleasant, though less familiar, cat is the Tonkinese, derived from crossbreeding Siamese and Burmese cats. The body type resultingly rests between

*The Tonk is a pleasant, biddable cat who happily accepts the attention and affection of household members.*

***Above and Opposite:*** *One pleasing attribute of the Tonk is his soft and silky coat, which can be any one of five shades of mink.*

these two breeds, not as svelte and elongated as the Siamese and less cobby than the Burmese. For persons who resist extremes, the Tonkinese is a pleasing middle-of-the-road purebred cat. It has been in existence since the 1960s. The Tonk's head is a modified wedge,

There's rarely a dull moment with a Tonkinese: these cats are fun to own (and care for).

longer than it is wide. A break at the nose is noticeable. The cheekbones are not prominent; muzzle is blunt, with a slight whisker break.

The coat is well-sheened and silky to the touch, of medium length. Color in the Tonk is very important. The body color is one of five shades of mink: natural mink; medium brown with lighter hues, with darker points; champagne mink, a buff cream with medium brown points; blue mink, a bluish gray with slate blue points; honey mink, described as a golden cream with an apricot cast, with ruddy brownish points; and platinum pink, a light silver-gray, with pewter gray points. Eye color—always aqua—complements every coat color. In personality, the Tonkinese is without competition. They are spontaneous and fun-loving with strong wills. Disciplinary soundness is firmly recommended. Grooming requires little more than a weekly once-over.

**Turkish Angora**

The Turkish Angora, or simply Angora, was revived by American cat fanciers. This breed (or the original breed) was thought to be extinct for many generations. The Angora cats of Turkey

*Turkish Angora. This beautiful specimen of a cat, with its sweet and tranquil temperament, is a cherished member of the cat world.*

are credited with progenerating today's Persian breed. Returning the favor graciously, Persians were used with other breeds to reincarnate the lost Ankara cat. Since the revival in the early 1960s, type has become stabilized and set. There is no denying the unique beauty of the Turkish

*The Turkish Angora is a responsive cat, known to be highly intelligent and very alert.*

Angora. Perhaps its most breathtaking feature is its coat. The coat is medium-long on the body but long at the ruff. Neck, belly and tail (full brush) are thickly coated. Tufts to the ears. Texture, fine and silky. The breed does not have a double coat like the Persian. Today the breed comes in many colors, in addition to pure white which is the color traditionally associated with Angora cats. Among the accepted colors are: black, blue, chocolate, lilac, red, tortie and calico, cream, blue tortie, chocolate tortie, lilac tortie, tabby (all colors), smokes and bi-colors. The Angora is a surprisingly trainable and biddable cat. It looks to its owner for attention and depends on a lot of time spent daily. Since the coat requires some brushing to keep clean, the Angora's persuasion towards humans is advantageous. The coat is not as long as

*The expressive almond-shaped eyes add to the appeal of the Angora.*

that of the Persian and the lack of undercoat makes grooming less of a chore. In addition to the Angora's uncompromising elegance, they are active cats who enjoy partaking in human activities. The number of Angoras is continually increasing as the breed usurps Persian and Himalayan fanciers alike.

A healthy kitten is alert and curious about its environment.

# Proper Accommodations

Necessary feline
accommodations include the
feeding dish and water bowl,
litter box and litter, and
scratching post and bed.
Ideally these items are
purchased before the new cat
is brought home. Having the
home well prepared with all
necessary accommodations
and supplies makes for the
most easy, stressless new cat
introduction.

Feeding dishes and water
bowls come in many
different shapes, sizes, and
colors, and are made of many
different materials. The most
recommended dishes and
bowls are those of stainless
steel or sturdy plastic, for
they invariably prove long
lasting and easy to clean.
Dishes and bowls should be
cleaned and sanitized daily.
A dish or bowl which suffers

*Remember that the newcomer to
your family needs time to adjust to
his new home.*

a deep scratch is best replaced, as the crevice can become a breeding ground for bacteria.

The litter box is also best composed of sturdy plastic that is easily cleaned. The interior box is best a smooth, hard surface, which prevents bacterial growth and thereby cuts back on odor. The box should be placed in a rather seclusive place, but which is easy and quick for the cat to reach. During the early stages of ownership, the cat will likely be kept in a restricted area with the box. If possible, it is best that the litter box remain in its first location. If the box is moved, it may be best to restrict the new area until you are certain that the cat will use the litter box in the new location. Typically, however, there is little problem in changing the location of the box once that cat is fully litter box trained.

The scratching post and bed may present some conflict and consideration for the owner. Despite the cat's inherent need to claw objects, and despite its affinity for cozy corners, owner-provided scratching posts and beds are not welcomed accessories of the

*Most domestic cats have an affinity for cozy little hideaways.*

*A hooded basket such as this is comfortable, durable, and offers its occupant a secure haven he can think of as his very own.*

*Today's cat lacks for nothing as far as accommodations are concerned. Miniaturized versions of "people" furniture are but one of the amenities available for cats.*

cat. Much research has been performed in an attempt to determine just why a cat selects certain objects to claw, and researchers realize that the first to contrive a proven 100-percent effective scratching post will indeed be a wealthy, well-rewarded researcher. The two most consistent findings on why a cat prefers to claw a given object reveal that scent and texture in part determine the desirability of many objects for many cats. In other words, cats seem to claw objects because they smell right or they feel right, possibly both. However, these findings are in no way conclusive, for too many cats do not adhere to these principles, and most cats disobey them on occasion. Nonetheless, a scratching post is most definitely a worthy part of the home accommodations. The scratching post should be placed at a location which is always accessible to the cat. The key to getting your cat to use its scratching post is observation. If the cat does not claw the post but claws

*If your cat has to be confined, make sure that the cage enclosure is large enough to accommodate him comfortably.*

*Left: Nothing escapes the attention of a cat: they love to explore everything in their environment. Opposite: Cat carriers are invaluable when it comes to transporting your cat.*

at another location, try moving the post to the cat's chosen location. If this too fails, try adding to the post some of the same material which you find the cat clawing. Try also adding the same scent which you feel prevails at the cat's chosen location, i.e.,foot tracks, fresh-washed hands, etc. You may also try showing the cat how ideal the post is for scratching by placing its paws on the post and pulling them downward, but in the end there is no guarantee that your cat will use its post. With torn curtains, plucked pillows, and shredded silk the risk, it makes good sense to give your cat the benefit of the doubt and to try the scratching post.

Beds, like posts, are often refused by the feline. Also like posts, however, they have definite advantages to their use, and owners are therefore encouraged to offer the cat a bed of its own. Probably the first reason why beds fail is that owners fail to

consider their cat's preferences when initially placing them. Cats enjoy the security and surveillance afforded a high place, and cats love warmth. There is little doubt then that atop the refrigerator and atop the stove are the two most common sleeping places for the cat. Of course, it is quite impossible to place the bed atop the stove, and usually undesirable to place it atop the refrigerator and at many other of the cat's chosen locations, but compromise may still be in order. Placing the bed beside a heat duct, ideally near a window, can often be to the liking of a cat. This setting can be further enhanced by placing the bed atop a box or footstool and thereby adding elevation. This suggestion is of course but an example and may not be recommended for all cats. Placing the bed, like encouraging the use of the scratching post, requires observation of the cat. Notice the cat's preferred sleeping quarters, note their possible desirable features,

*Left:* A kitten should not be left unsupervised. *Opposite:* This cat hideaway also doubles as a scratching device.

*A seemingly innocuous play item like a piece of ribbon can cause harm if it is chewed upon. Provide your pet with safe play objects.*

***Opposite:*** *A cat's behavior alternates between spurts of highly charged activity and periods of quiet contemplation.*

*Wanting your new cat to feel welcome does not mean that you must give it free reign of your home.*

when such action would be appropriate. Rather, the cat's biological make-up dictates ample rest before and after the high-intensity outbursts which characterize hunting and play. Of course, cats which are not provided with adequate opportunity for such outbursts will still lounge restfully; such behavior is instinctive and cannot be eliminated, for internally the cat is still preparing for that long-awaited change to expend an immediate, high quantity of energy. Unfortunately, cats which are not provided with adequate opportunity can become bored and lethargic, contributing to the fallacy of their being lazy. Therefore, it is the owner's responsibility to provide the cat with daily opportunity to expend its energy in a feline way.

Exercise is most beneficial to the cat, and it is unfortunate that so many owners today see their cat only as a lounging house ornament, needing only a daily feed and an occasional pet. Exercise helps tone the muscles and circulate the blood, thus in effect also conditioning the coat and skin and internal organs. Exercise regulates the appetite and contributes to good digestion and absorption of food. Exercise also relieves stress and makes for a happier, more contented cat.

As stated, providing

*All cats appreciate the opportunity to snooze undisturbed in a warm, sunny nook.*

*If a cat is provided with items that amuse and occupy him, he may be less inclined to explore areas that are off-limits.*

exercise for the cat is very different than providing exercise for the dog. To begin with most cats abhor the leash, and in truth a long leisurely walk is not the feline's natural way to exercise. If however, no other method of exercise is available, and if the cat approves, then walks on a lead can help satisfy the feline's need to exercise. More preferable would be the construction or purchase of a cat box and outdoor pen.

A cat box is really no definite article but can be any number of constructions that elicit activity in the cat. These boxes can be constructed by simply cutting medium-sized holes (large enough for the cat to pass through) into several cardboard boxes and then sealing the boxes together. The same can be done with wooden crates to provide a more durable construction. Similar constructions of sturdy, parasite–resistant plastic can often be found at pet shops, or if not can usually be easily ordered. Cat boxes, simple or elaborate, encourage the cat to jump, pounce, climb, and

*This head study illustrates the cat's keen alertness, a quality universal to all cats.*

otherwise exercise. Toys can be put into the boxes and the owner can also play with the cat while it is in its boxes, perhaps dangling a string or toy mouse. The outdoor pen is not an option for everyone, but owners with even a small patio or garden are encouraged to construct or purchase an enclosed pen in which branches (real or artificial) and other climbing posts, as well as steps, hanging toys, and other

*Just like people, cats have varied tastes and preferences.*

*Properly accommodating and caring for your cat can make for a very contented pet.*

*If you want your pet to enjoy the great outdoors, you should provide him with an outdoor exercise pen rather than letting him roam free.*

exercise-eliciting objects are placed. The outdoor pen, if properly constructed, can satisfy even the strongest feline desire to be outdoors and yet assure the owner of the cat's safety and well-being.

In addition to providing a cat box and exercise pen, cat owners are encouraged to spend quality play time with their cat. A myriad of cat toys can be found at your local pet shop, and safe make-shift toys of yarn and other materials can be easily created. It takes but little of your time and, in the end, providing your cat with adequate opportunity to exercise adds greatly to the rewards of cat ownership: the well-exercised cat is the better conditioned, healthier looking, happier cat.

## INDOOR -VS- OUTDOOR

Indoor versus outdoor, the decision to let your cat roam, is a serious, major decision, deserving of good thought and consideration. With all this talk about exercise, the owner may feel that allowing his cat access to the great outdoors will lead to a healthier, happier cat. Though in times past, such may have been the case, allowing the cat to roam in today's world brings grave

danger to the cat and questions the responsibility of the owner. Besides the obvious dangers of automobiles, cat-hating neighbors, and cat-loving

*Allowing your cat up on your furniture is strictly a matter of personal choice.*

canines, swimming pools, outside electrical wires, disease-carrying vermin, children, and other roaming cats also pose very real, life-endangering threats.

Therefore, allowing the cat access to the outdoors should not be a free given. Some owners argue that the cat belongs outdoors, deserves its freedom. In truth, the cat kept indoors and given ample opportunity for exercise, as already discussed, is by far the happier cat, who will likely enjoy more years of life, guarded against the numerous dangers of the outdoors. Of course, the decision of whether or not to let the cat roam rests on the owner's shoulders.

Responsible owners must weigh the factors, including their own conscience, the sanctity of wildlife, and the overpopulation of cats due largely to roaming cats, and cast his final decision. This author hopes that the decision is for the best of the cat, the owner, and all other factors considered.

**Opposite and Right:**
*Purebred or mongrel, adult or kitten, the cat is a creature of great interest and appeal.*

*Cats are notably intelligent animals and, as such, make good candidates for training.*

# Training the Cat

## LESSON ONE: THE SAND BOX

As with humans, cats receive their first lessons from their parents. Relying much on the instincts of her litter, the queen conducts the family's first training session quite early on. Fortunately for the humans, kittens pass LITTER BOX 101 before they enter into their new homes at six to eight weeks. Cats are naturally clean creatures which not only understand the purpose of the litterbox, but also learn to bury their "business" quite automatically.

For the kitten's second parents, its new owners, litterbox training consists of the simple matter of introducing the cat to the box. It will likely explore the area, ascertain the quality of the sand and plastic, their scent and feel. Keep the litterbox in an easily accessible area and do not

*It is best to establish the parameters of where your pet is allowed while the animal is still young.*

move it from the selected location.

Some less attentive kittens or stray adult cats require a relative degree of litterbox training. To housetrain a cat,

*Training can be tiresome, so keep training sessions reasonably short.*

place it in the litterbox after a good feeding; the pressure exerted on the digestive tract by a full stomach will stimulate the cat to excrete. Kittens will respond more quickly to this pressure, relieving themselves shortly after each feeding. Adult cats may require a half-hour or more before feeling the need to eliminate. Despite such differences, the cat should be placed in the litterbox immediately following each meal, which suggests to the cat what the actual purpose of this sand box is. If the cat does not perform as desired, but chooses to wander about, play in the litter and kick sand at its hopeful audience, don't allow it to leave and restrict its dalliance as much as possible. Limit the cat's area of straying if it refuses to stay in the box. As soon as signs of evacuation are noticeable, gently pick the cat up and place it in its litter box. Pat the sand to get

*Some cats are nonplused by physical handling and will not take kindly to the notion, while others may even welcome it.*

the cat's attention. Do not attempt to instruct the cat by example, since most cats will not respond to having an owner manipulate their paws through the sand. A cat will perceive this as an inane sand box game, and not be amused or interested.

After the cat excretes, lavish praise and a small treat, if desired, are appropriate. If training proves unsuccessful, try moving the box to a new location, perhaps one that is more remote or private. If a mishap occurs, firm correction is appropriate, but the owner must be careful not to overdo the correction; be firm and corrective, not vociferous and irrational, and your cat will be more responsive and tolerant of correction.

Some owners have experienced fully housetrained adult cats stop burying their waste, or

*Cats are very individualistic. Therefore, their response to a training program can vary.*

boycott the litterbox altogether. If an accident occurs once or twice,

consider that the cat may be suffering from a condition. Cystitis, for example, can force a cat to urinate frequently, and suddenly. Dribbling cats and other offenders should be examined by a veterinarian. Have the cat inspected carefully for outward signs. However, if all is normal, such insurrection may be your pet's ploy for attention. When a cat refuses to cover refuse, it may be caused by the cat's laziness, especially if the cat sees you clean up after it before it has a chance to "get off the box." Give the cat a chance to execute its excretion-covering ritual: this kitty rite is an evolutionary urge shared by all cats, great and small, as well as the cat's ancient ancestors. The great cats, lions and tigers, may or may not cover their waste—they also are less manageable in housetraining sessions. An adult male lion likely does

*A carpet-covered cat pedestal that also serves as a scratching post is a useful item to have.*

not bury his feces, but instead deposits it in a prominent place, like a hilltop, to mark his territory, a subtle indicator to other males passing that this is his domain. If your adult cat leaves his feces uncovered

*When it comes to training your cat, be reasonable in your expectations of what you want him to do.*

when you get a new cat, this territorial instinct may be your cat's media to admonish the new cat that this house is his domain.

## FOLLOW MY LEAD

Lesson number two in training the cat is "never expect your cat to be a dog." Dogs instinctively respond to lead training, as well as to basic obedience instruction. Cats, on the other less shackled paw, must be bribed to comply to man's wishes. Collars on cats do not often pose a problem for

owners. Some cats will accept the collar with nary a complaint, while others will contort their bodies and nearly strangulate themselves trying to free themselves from the "omnipresent constraining device."

Before engaging your cat in leash training sessions, decide how important this kind of training is. Do not attempt to teach your cat useless, party tricks for fleeting amusement; if leash training is just a novelty for you, you are better off not bothering, or buying a dog.

For those committed to lead training, there are some basic steps to follow. A leash-trained cat makes a great companion, more obliging and cooperating than the average feline, and likes the time spent outdoors with its

*Permitting a cat to have access to an open window is courting a potential disaster. Any number of things could capture the cat's curiosity and thus entice him to "make a break for it."*

**Above:** The Bengal, a relatively new breed of cat, can be a good candidate for training if he is trained in a patient and persistent manner. **Opposite:** Just as cats differ in personality, so do they differ in their capacity to be successfully trained.

owner. The author encourages this kind of training, since it is advantageous to allow your cat to get fresh air regularly.

*The cat is a remarkably agile and graceful creature.*

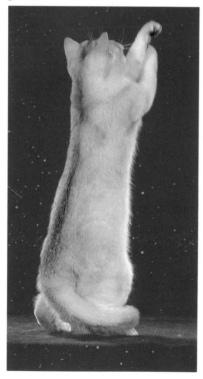

We are naturally assuming that your cat is an indoor cat, since outdoor urban areas are too ominous and dangerous for domestic cats to roam. Leash training is also advantageous to owners who favor weekend expeditions and want their cat to come along. While traveling in a moving vehicle, however, a cat must be kept in a crate for its safety and the driver's.

The best candidates for leash training are shorthaired cats, since longhaired breeds have not responded to this type of training as well as shorthaired breeds. There is little mystery for this situation. Lead training requires that a cat be placed in a harness, and longhaired cats almost invariably find this device uncomfortable. Additionally, certain longhaired breeds, despite their plush, warm coats, are not terribly fond of the outdoors. Persians, Himalayans, and Ragdolls

*Training a kitten can be easier than training an adult cat.*

*Cats are intelligent animals, capable of retaining what they have learned.*

for instance are recent manmade creations and do not take to the outdoors like many shorthaired breeds, or even the rustic longhaired Maine Coon. Maine Coons, incidentally, have been successfully lead trained on occasion, but these happy campers prefer to experience the great outdoors minus the nylon vest. Among the cats which most often are lead trained are the Abyssinian, Siamese and American and British Shorthairs. It should be submitted here, however, that any cat, shorthaired or longhaired, purebred or moggy, can be lead trained with the proper technique, commitment and patience.

The necessary harness should be constructed of either nylon or a soft leather. Pet shops and supply houses stock cat harnesses. Do not buy a dog harness from your grocery store and try to train your cat with it; they are designed differently and should not be used. The leash should be about six feet in length. Introduce the leash and harness to the cat as toys in the home. The animal's familiarity with these accoutrements will ease the training process. After the cat has made friends with his nylons, place the harness around the cat. Since cats pride themselves on their originality and individuality, the author cannot predict your cat's reaction at this point. Ideally the cat will not be bothered by the harness and act normal. Other cats, however, pretend to be lame, dumb and/or in a state of shock. The author has watched perfectly normal, though terribly creative, cats go completely haywire when placed in a harness for the first time. Conniptions and extended delirium tremens

*First and foremost, the cat is an independent animal that cannot be made to do anything against its will.*

mark the sign of the true feline actor and no matter how taken you are by your cat's performance, ignore it since it is but a bluff. You can either attempt to restrain the cat or wait it out—understandably paralysis just for fun cannot last too long, even though the cat is admired in the animal world for its patience and persistence. Perhaps if your cat perceives this situation as dire and dread-related, it will lie on the floor, staring blankly for an hour, but more than likely its boredom will override its persistence.

Assuming the cat has been successfully harnessed, is conscious, and reasonably

*The more time you spend with your cat, the better you will know its moods.*

willing to cooperate, we continue by attaching the leash to the harness. Be sure the cat is securely in the harness, though not unduly tight. Let the cat meander about the house for about 15 or 20 minutes, dragging its leash around, trying to act normal. Bribe the cat to come to you by calling it and offering a treat. Once you have hold of the leash attempt to walk a few steps through the room. Don't expect the cat to cooperate wholeheartedly with the proceedings. Accomplishing a few steps for a first lesson is a braggable feat. Dragging the cat, tugging and pulling at the lead, will never do. Talk to the cat and walk next to it. Eventually, maybe, the cat will grasp the idea that you want to walk alongside one another. By the second and third period, you should have the cat cooperating enough to walk around inside the house for a little

*It goes without saying that a cat is highly worthy of praise—and, some say, reward—when it performs upon command.*

while. When a cat is tired or bored with the leash thing, it will simply refuse to continue, instantly becoming a feline paper weight—dead weight cannot (and should not) be tugged around since no learning can go on at this point. After a while the cat will be ready to take outside. If the cat has never been outside, it will not be much encouragement, since many indoor cats are frightened out of their minds of the outdoors. Eventually, the cat will look forward to getting outside on its leash and will comply to walking you. This is a great outing for exercise purposes, particularly for portent felines who live from meal to nap to meal. Incidentally, cats usually decide their own path and set the pace. Owners looking for a jogging companion or a partner for a once-around-the-park walk should have considered a retriever before beginning this chapter. If you do have a cat willing to take to the park on a Sunday afternoon, always be ready to pick the cat up when an ex-cat fancier comes briskly by with his well-paced retriever. Lastly, it is more important than ever that your cat have all its vaccinations updated if you intend to have it outside near other lead-trained animals.

*Whether your pet is a purebred or mongrel is of no great significance in the success of training the animal.*

Allow your kitten ample
opportunity for playtime.

grooming itself and you will experience the cat's deep need for independence. All cats have different personalities, although members of the same breed

*Independent and aloof, the cat does not need the same type of approval that some other kinds of pets—notably, the dog—seek.*

often exhibit similar personality quirks and attitudes towards humans. Burmese, for instance, are more playful than most cats; Himalayans are highly independent; Russian Blues highly devoted to their owners; Havana Browns soft spoken and pawed.

Outgoing cats generally are easier to train and more amenable to attention than timid or shy cats. If you have chosen your breed of cat with the intention of training it, you should have little problem engaging your cat in sessions. With any cat, its attention span must be considered. Cats are very bright, and like bright children, get bored very easily and may attempt to find new ways of pleasing you. Some cats are natural hams and love attention, these very eager cats are often very trainable. Sometimes too much verve can be a drawback. Such cats

*Though they may not be the easiest animals to train, cats, by their very nature, offer unique companionship that is sought after by many.*

were likely the bullies of their litter and enjoy getting their own way much of the time.

As we have said, the best way to get a cat to perform a trick or task or to obey a command is to bribe it! You must maintain your cat's attention—any way you can. Much more so than dogs, cats will ignore their owners, especially when their owners are trying too hard, or simply when it pleases the cat to do so. Once the cat learns that executing a given/spoken chore will yield a treat, it will perform that trick. With any luck, the cat will continue to obey that command after you have ceased providing tidbits.

Some of the most popular and successful commands and tricks include: Come,

***Above:*** *American Curl.* ***Opposite:*** *Egyptian Mau. Every breed of cat can rightly stake its own claim to a charm and appeal all its own.*

*Don't expect that your cat will respond to your every command, especially if he is outdoors, amidst a number of things which can capture his attention.*

Up or Stand, Sit or Stay, jumping though a hoop.

To teach a cat the "Come" command, place the cat on the opposite side of the room. Pointing at the cat, speak "Come" firmly, and then bring your arm down to your side, now pointing to the floor. It may be necessary to coax the cat with a morsel of something delightful. Praise the cat when it finally comes. Repeat the sequence, beginning by pointing at the cat, etc. If your cat refuses to comply whatsoever to this command, do not lose heart and be persistent;    it could

be that your cat simply resents being pointed at, since in most circles this is a rude gesture.

To coerce the cat to stand on its hind legs, present a treat on a long stick and the cat will stand up to reach it. Perhaps use the command "Up" or "Stand" to indicate your intentions.

Of course the easiest of all cat tricks, is the "sit" or "stay," at least when the cat is already in a sedentary position. In an equally firm voice, say either command (choose one and stick with it). Pleased that your cat has

**The Singapura, known for its adaptability.**

listened to its commanding owner, reward the cat. To lengthen the sit period, extend the amount of time before you give the cat its treat. If nothing ever becomes of this command, it

*Familiarizing yourself with your cat's vocalizations will help you to better understand its needs.*

could be that the cat hasn't noticed your speaking or recognize your didactic or instructive tone of voice. In these cases, the cat is merely hanging out for a treat.

Hoop jumping will require the best treats you can afford. Fortunately pet food companies continually improve on the extravagance and feline appeal of their treats, so cat training gets that much easier (and more expensive). Jumping through a loop is but an extension of the cat walking through the hoop. You must reward the cat as it walks towards you through the hoop. Gradually you can lift the hoop from the floor and the cat's step will naturally transform into a mini-leap and then a bigger jump and finally quite a pounce through the ring. Since this is work for a cat, treats may not ever be eliminated from the proceeding. You can also work boxes into the trick by

*If your cat's attention begins to wander, stop the training session imme-diately. Don't make training into a chore.*

having the cat walk across the two boxes, with the hoop in the middle. Gradually you separate the boxes and the cat will leap from one box (through the loop) to the other. The lucky owner's cat will find all this attention fun and cooperate grandly with the diversion. Professional cat trainers use treats in performance and their cats often jump eight to ten feet from one podium to another, through a hoop or grabbing a treat from the trainer's hand. Whether or not you will be able to accomplish such a feat is doubtful since this kind of training requires long hours, commitment and years of experience.

***Above:*** *American Shorthair.* ***Opposite:*** *Oriental Shorthair. By and large, cats are emotionally sensitive creatures; their training must be approached accordingly.*

# Grooming and Hygiene

All cats, longhaired and shorthaired, require grooming on a regular basis, ideally every day. Many cat owners don't see the need for grooming because they know that their cat must groom itself about 20 times a day, which is true. Yet, the cat's inherent meticulous grooming habits in no way subtract from the importance of the owner's grooming. Grooming, which entails the use of brushes and combs, helps keep the skin and coat healthy and glistening by distributing natural oils, stimulating circulation, and

removing dirt and debris.

The cat's relatively small size makes positioning the cat for grooming relatively easy; either the owner's lap or standard table work just fine. Under the cat should be placed a white cloth, which will catch the falling hair and

**Opposite and Right:** *It is up to you to keep your cat looking its very best.*

*Above:* The Himalayan requires regular combing. *Opposite:* The Sphynx must be especially safeguarded against skin irritations.

also assist in the detection of parasites: ticks and fleas, typically black or brown in color, will readily appear on the cloth should they drop off during the grooming session.

The cat should become accustomed to the grooming procedure at as early an age as possible. Most cats, if introduced to grooming at an early age, come to welcome the attention and time spent with their owner. Cats which experience their first grooming session after they are fully mature almost invariably resist the procedure and require much time and patience to prove to them that grooming is a pleasurable—not painful process. Daily grooming procedures can begin on the day after you bring your new kitten home. Of course, the first grooming sessions will

*Scratching can be a sign of flea infestation. Check your pet regularly for parasites.*

the lie, complete this first stage of grooming by again working the entire coat in the direction of its lie. Now comes the combing, which should be done in the same basic three-step manner as brushing—first combing the complete coat with its lie, then completely against it, and finishing with its lie. This entire process can be

performed separately with two different tooth-spaced combs, if you have the extra time and your cat has the extra patience. As a final step to the grooming procedure, a vigorous brushing with the lie of the coat gives the finishing touches.

Grooming the short hair requires less time but is no less important than the grooming of the longhair: as with the longhaired, daily grooming contributes immeasurably to the overall health of the shorthaired cat. To begin, place the cat comfortably on a table or your lap, with a white cloth underneath to help in the detection of parasites. Essentially all that is required is a thorough brushing of the entire coat—

*The time you spend grooming your cat is but a small price to pay for the enjoyment and satisfaction he gives you.*

on the upper body, underbody, and sides—in the direction in which the coat lies. The groomer must be gentle when brushing around the tail, face, inner legs, for these are sensitive parts. For most thorough grooming, the groomer may wish to

*Grooming can be easy or difficult, depending upon the condition of the cat's coat.*

follow the three-step brushing procedure as discussed for the longhaired cat, or for a quick addition follow the one-step brushing with a one-step combing. For the polishing touch, the coat can be given a brisk rub with a chamois or silk cloth.

## BATHS

Unquestionably, most cats never require a bath, and most that do so typically have their bathing needs satisfied by a dry-type bath. Yet there are always those few exceptions which require the full-scale wet and lathery bath. Unless your cat is a show cat or becomes plagued with parasites, bathing is

*__Opposite:__ The room in which your pet is bathed should be free of drafts.*

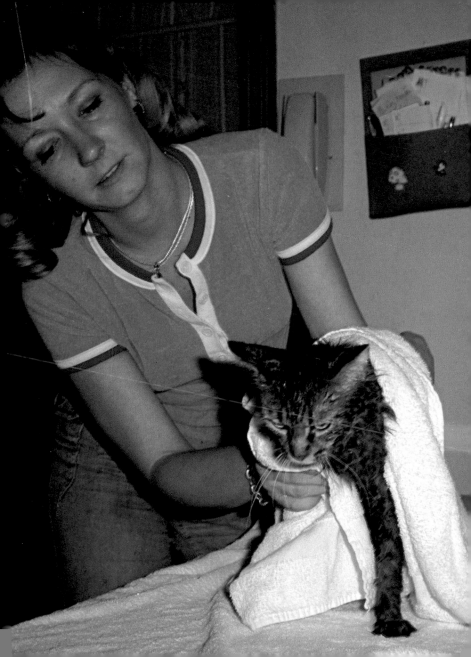

*Opposite:* The British Shorthair requires a modest amount of grooming. *Above:* The Egyptian Mau, another easy-to-groom cat.

variety of different types, each of which is specially suited to fulfill a specific feline bathing need. Some dry baths commonly available include those that treat flea and tick problems, clean the coat and skin, condition the coat, eliminate minor odors. A dry bath can be easily incorporated into a

*It is best to start grooming early in kittenhood.*

more an option than a need. For routine bathing, such as is required for show or treating minor flea problems, dry baths most often suffice. Most dry baths, available at local pet shops, need only be sprinkled on, allowed to set, and then brushed out after a given time period. Dry baths, like most pet products, are available in a

*Above:* Regular grooming is the key to keeping your cat's coat and skin in tiptop shape. *Opposite:* Kittens, especially, need careful supervision.

daily grooming should it be needed. Specific directions for the bath's use should be found on the product and should be followed exactly.

If a wet bath is needed, as might be the case for treating a serious skin condition or parasite infestation, or for eliminating a mega-stinky odor, the bather be advised: Beware! If the cat is mature (over one year of age) and is going to receive its first bath, the bather should protect himself with high-fitting

***Above and Opposite:*** *Whether your cat is a longhair or a shorthair, it is easy to recognize a coat that is in poor condition: It will have a decidedly dull appearance.*

gloves to guard against cat scratches. A second person should be available to help hold the cat while the first achieves the lather. Perhaps most important is quickness: invariably the cat is hating the moment, so finish without delay. Of course, be thorough, especially when rinsing the lather from the coat; left over lather can dry the coat and skin and cause flaking and possibly infection. If you are at all uncertain about giving your cat its first wet bath, you can ask your veterinarian or a professional groomer to provide the service for you. As a general rule, bathe the cat, or have the cat bathed, as infrequently as possible. Excessive bathing, regardless of the intention of the product, can eventually damage the coat and skin and lead to numerous complications.

*Nothing prevents a cat from shedding, but regular grooming can reduce the quantity of hair that is left on household furnishings.*

## ADDITIONAL HYGIENIC NEEDS

The eyes, ears, and nose are susceptible to injury and infection, and responsible owners should check these parts during each grooming session. If any disorder is noted, prompt proper care is imperative, as even a minor problem of the eyes, ears or nose can quickly lead to a serious condition.

The eyes are often the first sign of illness or ill feeling: if the cat does not feel well, you can almost invariably notice it in the cat's eyes, which may appear dull, listless, distant. Additionally, the eyes are prone to receive foreign objects. Foreign objects, which may be as small as a speck, typically cause redness to the white of the eye and watery discharge from the eye. Infection, which is often but not

*After your pet has been outdoors, he should be checked for fleas and other pesky parasites.*

*Routine visual inspections of your cat's eyes, ears, and nose are part of a proper grooming regimen.*

necessarily the result of a foreign object, shows similar signs but may also cause pus to form around the rim of the eye. All these conditions require immediate veterinary care. Day-to-day debris, which often accumulates at the corner of the eye, should be removed with a soft cotton swab, moistened with sterile water or mineral oil. The cleaned eye should be checked regularly for the next few days to make

***Above:*** *Grooming not only maintains your cat's best appearance, but it also enhances the animal's overall well-being.* ***Opposite:*** *These rather unlikely pals share a favorite pastime: both are known for their penchant for preening.*

*To some fanciers, nothing beats the look and feel of a longhaired feline, even if it means a bit more work in the grooming department.*

accumulations often lead to gum disease and tooth decay. Longhaired-cat owners should be aware that the cat's hair can become entangled in the teeth, later decaying and possibly causing foul-breath and gum disease.

Like the eyes, nose, ears, and teeth, the claws of the cat need to be checked regularly. Typically the cat's claws require little care from the owner, as cats meticulously hone the claws by scratching and "chewing" them on a daily basis. However, weak, brittle claws can be a sign of poor nutrition, and overgrown claws may require that the owner intervene where the cat is failing in its personal hygienic needs, perhaps by filing or clipping the tips of the claws. Most often, only older cats will require such intervention, but the owner should take the daily moment to make sure that all

Chipped teeth can be a sign of poor diet, often lacking in calcium or phosphorus. Tartar and plaque accumulation should be removed as necessary by a trained professional, as these

is well with the claws, and while inspecting them should also check the feet and foot pads for foreign objects, matted fur, tar, and other potentially harmful things.

Many owners consider having their cat declawed, which is the surgical procedure by which the cat's claws are permanently removed. Declawing as a practice raises many questions, some of which are ethical. Most feline authorities believe that declawing is a poor practice that both physically and psychologically harms the cat. The basis of their argument is the high value of the claws to the cat. The cat naturally uses its claws to play, hunt, and defend itself. Though cats are adaptable creatures, removing their

*The decision to declaw (or not to) rests heavily on every cat owner's shoulders, for without its claws, a cat is virtually defenseless.*

claws necessarily inhibits these and other important activities. Cats with claws removed cannot climb, which is a major form of feline exercise; and some reports show that cats with claws removed are more likely to bite, since they feel more helpless, defenseless without their claws. Owners who support the declawing procedure generally rely on convenience as their only argument. In the end, however, the decision of whether or not to have the cat's claws removed rests with the owner. This author feels that declawing is generally a senseless procedure, but does believe that if the cat's claws are the only deterrent or detriment to a human-to-feline relationship, then the claws might better be removed, for a feline, without its claws, in a safe and well-providing home is surely better off than a feline, with its claws, roaming the street or filling a shelter.

**Left:** *A unique quality of the cat's claws is that they are retractable.*
**Opposite:** *Turkish Van.*

**Left, Below, and Opposite:**
Indoors or outdoors, solo or with mom, a kitten exudes an air of alert anticipation.

*A mother cat's milk provides the young kittens with the essential nutrients needed for healthy development.*

and safe relationship.

The newly arrived family member may be upset from its traveling. Depending on the kitten, its personality, breed, and adaptability, it may or may not assert itself, resisting the temptation of an unexplored wilderness. Kittens are prized for their curiosity and verve for exploration. Allow the kitten to inspect the area you've designated. Do not overhandle the kitten since holding and petting the cat are irresistible to all cat lovers, six years old or sixty years old. The kitten will require very consistent attention since it is prone to trouble and messes.

Introduce the kitten to its bed, food dish, and litter pan at the appropriate times. Rely upon the guidelines of the breeder or seller to determine what the kitten should be eating. Do not change the cat's diet drastically right away since this will cause a digestive upset in all likelihood.

Protecting the floor with a polyethylene sheet or a similar plastic covering will

*A kitten exploring the pleasures and treasures of the outdoors under the expert tutelage of his parent.*

help to minimize soiling. Keep the kitten's area clean, particularly its eating area and its litterbox. The kitten's area is also best out of direct sunlight and away from any potential hazards. Kitchens are a common choice for the new kitten but remember that this room is subject to high traffic and a great number of potentially dangerous situations. Stoves, electrical cords, cabinets,

*Felines can be remarkably demonstrative in their affection for one another.*

*This kitten displays the irresistible sweetness and innocence of kittenhood.*

refrigerators, dishwashers, clothes dryers, etc., are all worthy of exploration and an unrestrained kitten will set out to conquer each and every appliance, nook and cranny of your kitchen.

The kitten should be introduced to the litterbox after its meal. Quite instinctively the kitten will adopt this designated area to perform its natural duty. Cat owners bask in the convenience of housing some of God's cleanest creatures. If you notice your new kitten preening itself, washing its face and paws, you can be assured that the cat is accepting its new environment as home.

Consider also the temperature of the room

*Given the proper care and attention, your new kitten will readily become accustomed to his new home.*

which the kitten is inhabiting. While a hardy long-coated kitten will be fine during the colder months without additional heating, many short-coated cats require some supplemental heat. Pet shops sell heaters especially designed for pet use which can be kept in or near a kitten's sleeping area.

Once the kitten has settled into its new home, the time arrives when it can be permitted to see the rest of

**Above, Below, and Opposite:** *Each kitten is an individual with its own endearing habits and winning ways.*

*Development levels—from kittenhood to adulthood—can vary from one breed of cat to another.*

separately. Spats and squabbles most frequently erupt at meal times, and a kitten is hardly capable of holding his own to your hungry Saint Bernard. Introduction to other animals must be undertaken with caution and patience. Kitten encountering adult cat must be planned—do not force the cats' acquaintance, nor let it happen by chance without supervision. While cats are not the most gregarious of animals, they do not despise the company of their own kind. Intact males will be the most aggressive feline acquaintances of your kitten. Living together in relative harmony is achieved with a little snarling and scratching, even if the two cats will never be bosom buddies.

Provided that your kitten hasn't already nurtured a prejudice against the canine species (i.e., had a bad run-in with a dog), likely it will accept the dog with little

its indoor universe and meet the other occupants of the house. If you have a dog in your home already, it is wise to feed the two animals

*With time, love, and patience, your kitten can become an affectionate and devoted feline companion.*

hesitation, once it gets over its initial fear. Dogs are simple creatures and will instinctively want to play with the new kitten. A large dog, frothing and fumbling to roll on the carpet with a tiny kitten, will surely age the kitten a few months. These potentially dangerous encounters need close supervision and intervention. Human mediation is advisable when introducing the canine and feline species. Some dogs, however, are not inclined to welcome a cat into their household, or may not be willing to accept a second cat as willingly as they did the first. Most dogs are naturally protective animals and do not limit the boundaries of

**Below and Opposite:** Cats, be they purebred or mongrel, are among the most popular domestic pets.

*Proper socialization is an important factor in the transition from kittenhood to adulthood.*

disposition and usually take full advantage of the situation. Cats accept the protection and companionship of dogs, while still remaining uncompromisingly self-reliant creatures.

Feeding the kitten presents relatively few complications to the new owner. Continue feeding the kitten as recommended by the previous keeper, gradually altering the diet as you desire as time passes and the cat is more settled in. Kittens have big appetites for the diminutive sizes. Four or five meals per day are standard for a kitten under six months of age. Supplementing a canned food diet or a dry food diet

the area which they protect. Dogs often take cats under their wing, protecting them as they do the human members of the household. Cats are aware of the dog's subservient, servantile

*__Opposite:__ This Havana Brown embodies the mysterious aura that is part of the cat's unique appeal.*

with fresh meat and fish can prove advantageous, and also keep mealtimes interesting (a task quite easy to accomplish with kittens generally). Milk is a good source of calcium and can be fed to the kitten especially when providing fresh meat. Despite the non-kosher aspects of this type of feeding, meat is low in calcium and the fresh milk can compensate for some of the lost mineral. Be careful with milk, however, since some kittens suffer from diarrhea when they consume fresh milk.

**Below and Opposite:** *The cat owner can enrich his own life—and his cat's—by learning and accepting the basics of feline behavior.*

# Feeding and Nutrition

Properly feeding the feline demands a basic understanding of the cat's nutritional needs and biological constitution. Even if you rely on commercial cat foods, which typically provide a well-balanced diet, knowing the cat's carnivorous and highly specialized feeding behavior makes for safer, more effective feeding practices.

Cats are not dogs; they cannot do well on a diet based on their human owner's table dressings. Whereas dogs are omnivores, able to digest and utilize both plant and animal tissue, cats are carnivores in the utmost sense of the word. Cats not only cannot digest plant matter but have a protein requirement (30–40% of their diet) which is roughly twice as great as the dog's, making meat, fish, eggs, milk, and other animal products essential. The cat's

*Opposite and Right: A sound diet is one of the most important factors in the overall health of your cat.*

**Opposite *and Right:*** *It is up to you to maintain a healthy weight for your pet: moderation is the rule of thumb.*

inability to create synthetically some amino acids and other vital chemicals (again, unlike the dog and many other animals) means that only by receiving a diet rich in animal foodstuffs will the cat be nutritionally well provided. Additionally, the cat's poor ability to detoxify and eliminate many substances from its body makes feeding the right foods in the right amounts ever more vital; an example is surplus vitamin A, which the cat cannot excrete and will lead to vitamin A poisoning. Hence we see the need for feeding the feline a diet truly befitting the feline.

The key to feline nutrition is balance. Providing a variety of meat products, with added carbohydrates, vitamins and minerals, when necessary is the best feeding practice. In general, concentrate more on meats (the muscles of the animal) than on the glands, such as liver and kidneys. Glandular foods, though typically relished by the feline, are too high in some vitamins to be fed as a staple, and should be served occasionally. Most vegetables and cereals cannot be digested by the cat unless they are first cooked properly to begin their breakdown. Of course, the cat owner of today need not fret over the diet of their charge, for many quality products are easily available at pet shops and other pet suppliers everywhere. Still, though, balance is the key, which is best achieved though variety. The cat should receive a meat, poultry, fish, gland, and other animal-based food regularly. Of course, too much variety can lead to a fussy eater, but choosing a balance of five or six type foods and rotating them in a regular, predictable manner should provide a most nutritionally sound diet for your cat.

*Below: Domestication has somewhat altered what can be called the cat's natural diet. Opposite: Feeding bowls should be cleaned on a daily basis.*

prescribe supplements or other changes to the cat's diet. Don't discount other cat owners or your local pet shop proprietor, for these people are also valuable sources of information about feline feeding.

*The dietary needs of the adult cat are different from that of the kitten.*

## FOODSTUFFS

Proteins are primarily necessary for the construction and repair of tissue; they can also serve as energy sources should the cat require them. There are many different proteins, each created by a different assembly of amino acids, which are the true building blocks of the animal. The animal digests proteins, breaking them down into their respective amino acids, and then reconstructs the amino acids into the body materials it needs. As stated, cats cannot synthesize some amino acids, which makes feeding a balanced protein diet (a diet containing many different proteins) necessary. A proper diet for the average adult cat should contain roughly 30–40 percent protein. Kittens and indeed all still-growing cats require relatively more protein because they are constructing comparatively more tissue

*The mother cat's milk contains essential proteins, vitamins, and other nutrients.*

daily. Good sources of protein include meats, fish, poultry, commercial canned foods, milk, and eggs. Dairy products must be fed with discretion, for they can cause diarrhea if fed in excess. Foodstuffs such as corn, potatoes, and rice also contain substantial amounts of protein, but the cat cannot digest these foods unless they are first well cooked. Additionally, vegetables and cereals lack suitable quantities of many of the

Carbohydrates form the bulk of animals' dietary intake (as much as 60–80 percent); cats, however, require that their diet contain only 30–40 percent carbohydrates. Carbohydrates are typically inexpensive, and provide an excellent way to add calories to diet. Most commercial cat foods contain a substantial amount of carbohydrates, with canned foods typically containing the lowest amounts. Carbohydrates are abundantly found in sugars and starches; thus, dairy products, fruits, vegetables, and grains are all foods high in carbohydrates. Of course, the cat cannot properly digest most foods which are high in carbohydrates unless they are adequately cooked (or predigested by the prey). The carbohydrates found in commercial cat foods are almost invariably properly prepared and thus serve well the carbohydrate needs of the cat.

Vitamins and minerals are not food, but they are required by the cat in very specific amounts to maintain good health. Vitamins and minerals are typically not found abundantly in meat products. Cats in the wild acquire vitamins and minerals by consuming the

*The proper diet will "fuel" a kitten's energetic bursts of activity.*

*The prudent feeding of the right foods will help ensure that your cat is "just right"—neither too fat nor too thin.*

glands and organs, feathers and bones, and bowel contents of prey species. Domestic cats receive the necessary vitamins and minerals through a well-balanced diet. As stated, cats cannot synthesize most

***Above and Opposite:*** *All cats—no matter what their breed—share basic nutritional needs that must be met to keep them looking their best.*

vitamins and also cannot rid excess vitamins from their body. Therefore, the owner must be certain that the cat is receiving just the right amount of vitamins and minerals for its needs. By far the easiest way to do this is to feed quality commercial cat foods that are scientifically designed to meet the cat's nutritional needs. If you, the owner, wish to feed your cat homemade meals, you are encouraged to talk first with your veterinarian.

For the cat owner's general

*Opposite and Above:* Properly caring for your cat is largely a matter of common sense.

reference, a brief summary of the essential vitamins and minerals is provided.

Vitamin A assists in growth and nerve health, digestion and appetite, coat condition, and vision. It is abundantly found in such foods as egg yolks, carrots and corn, many glandular foods, green vegetables and grains.

The B-complex vitamins, including B1 or thiamine, B2 or riboflavin, B6 or pyridoxine, and B12, assist in growth and general good health, including the maintenance of most vital organs. B vitamins are found variously in meat, milk, yeast, fish, vegetables, and all other foods containing proteins.

Vitamin C, also called citric acid, is important to the general good health of the cat; cats, like humans, will develop scurvy if deficient in vitamin C. Vitamin C is found bountifully in many fruits (especially citrus fruits) and vegetables.

Vitamin D works in conjunction with calcium and phosphorus and assists the teeth and bones in the

*A well-fed cat is generally an active, playful cat.*

*The energy requirements of cats vary. Size, age, and overall state of health—all of these things can affect your cat's energy needs.*

absorption and utilization of calcium. If calcium supplementing is necessary, then likely the vitamin D ration will also need boosting. Excessive vitamin D, however, can result in bloody stools and depression, among many other symptoms. Vitamin D, in good quantity, is found in dairy products; it is also called the sunshine vitamin and can be absorbed through sunlight.

Vitamin E has been called the healing vitamin and does assist the healing process; it also enhances muscle tone, and is believed to assist in delivery and lactation (most pregnant queens should receive vitamin supplements at the recommendation of a veterinarian.)

Vitamin K assists in blood clotting, and thus also prevents anemia. Alfalfa meal provides a rich amount of vitamin K.

Other elements that assist the cat in his everyday life include panthothenic acid, folic acid, and choline. These

*City cat or country cat? A cat that is confined to a small apartment will probably expend less energy than his country cousin.*

## MINERALS

The primary minerals required of a cat that the owner need concern himself with are calcium, phosphorus, and iron. Other minerals, which are also necessary but almost invariably are found adequately in a well balanced diet, include iodine, sodium and magnesium. Calcium and phosphorus are essential to sound bones and teeth. Both calcium and phosphorus are found in

*Above and Below:* Vitamins and minerals play an important role in maintaining the good health of your cat. Your pet shop carries a tempting array of foodstuffs that provide these elements.

elements, though necessary, are required in such small amounts that the owner need not fret about them: these elements almost invariably are provided in a well-balanced diet. These elements are found variously in yeast, liver and other glandular foods, and crude molasses.

*In addition to eating right, your pet should receive regular veterinary attention to keep it looking and feeling its best.*

dairy products, and most quality cat foods have these minerals supplemented into the meal. Developing kittens and nursing queens have particularly high demands for calcium, and a breeder/veterinarian-prescribed diet should be followed for both of them. Iron is needed only in very small amounts, though a lack of iron can result in serious consequences, including anemia and anemia's many secondary conditions. Pregnant queens will likely need small quantities of iron supplements. Egg yolks, meats, and glandular foods are particularly high in iron.

# Essential Health Keeping

Keeping the cat healthy stands as a true desire of every responsible cat owner. Healthy by nature, cats demand little in the form of special care. Kittens, elderly cats, and sick cats, of course, require additional consideration from the owner, but even these felines typically prove easy–keep animals. Choosing a healthy cat from the onset is, of course, the first step in keeping your cat healthy; and from this point, regular veterinary care and awareness of the basic

*Successful pet ownership begins with the selection of a cat or kitten that is sound and healthy.*

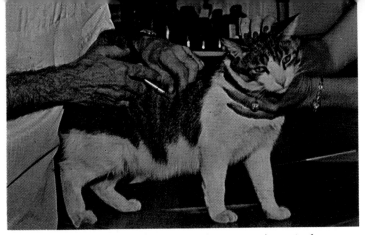

*Providing your cat with regular veterinary care is part of your responsibility as a pet owner.*

warning signs of illness are the keys to successful feline health keeping.

Choosing a healthy kitten or cat does not necessarily mean selecting a pure-bred feline—no more than it means choosing a street cat or household pet. Choosing a healthy cat means selecting a kitten or cat that comes from a healthy queen and an equally healthy tom. Both the tom and the queen should have all the necessary shots and be in excellent health at the time of breeding. Ideally both mother and father have a known ancestry of health and long life. Additionally, the kitten or cat you select from such an ideal breeding will have all its inoculations up-to-date at the time of purchase and will have been examined by a veterinarian.

Of course, not all cats and kittens are acquired under such obviously ideal conditions—many are unknowingly acquired from

*Felines that freely roam about can fall prey to a host of illnesses and accidents.*

a guarantee that the cat he chooses will be healthy throughout the duration of its life. Even cats chosen from the seemingly most ideal source can prove susceptible to a given condition or illness, and accidents, environmental conditions, and other uncontrollable factors can all contribute to the demise of a feline's health. This is not to say that a cat owner should expect his cat to suffer illness; it is to say that the cat owner should schedule regular veterinary check-ups and be alert to the basic warning signs of ill feline health.

such, while others are simply the result of poor or unplanned breedings, but which nonetheless are cats in need and deserving of a good home despite their inhibited start. Potential owners are not necessarily discouraged from keeping a kitten or cat from dubious health origins but are cautioned that there may be a greater likelihood of ill health for the cat.

The potential owner is reminded that there is never

Choosing a veterinarian is almost as important—some may argue more important—than choosing the cat itself. The veterinarian, more so than any other human in the cat's world, can properly inspect the cat's health, diagnose problems and conditions, and prescribe remedies for their rectification. Ideally, your cat's veterinarian is chosen before the purchase of your cat. One way to select a veterinarian is to visit all the local vets in your area and choose one with whom you are comfortable and who demonstrates a particular affinity for felines. Immediately following the purchase of your cat, you should bring it and all its health records to your chosen vet for review. There should be a clause in your buyer's contract which states that if the cat is not deemed acceptable for any health reasons by *your* vet then the cat may be returned within a given, stated time after purchase. Your vet will review the cat and its health records, prescribe all necessary vaccinations and/or inoculations, and even assist you in determining the proper diet and other helpful courses of action if you so ask. You and your vet should

With its curiosity and agility, a cat has the knack of getting itself into just about any spot imaginable.

*Given the proper care, your cat can enjoy years of companionship with you.*

A cat that eats zestfully, plays jubilantly, displays a healthy coat and sound body, and in general acts contentedly, almost invariably enjoys good health. Change, sudden and severe, is one of the surest signs of ill health. A cat which stops eating for several days, a cat which now hides for a better part of the day, or a cat which urinates profusely or has chronic loose stools, is a cat likely suffering from some ill condition. Successful treatment largely depends on expedient diagnosis and treatment. The cat owner, the daily observer of the cat, holds the greatest responsibility for noting signs of ill health and seeing to it that they receive proper care. The ten key signs of ill condition for which every cat owner should be aware are:

1. Sudden and lasting temperament changes; over-excitement, excessive shyness

then plan a veterinary routine, which for an adult cat is often once or twice a year, but which for kittens and elderly cats may be more frequent.

## SIGNS AND SYMPTOMS

Cats communicate their general condition to the observant owner every day.

*A change in your cat's appearance and/or behavior can be an indication that the animal is not well.*

*Kittens are fragile little creatures that should be handled with care.*

coat luster, eye clarity, muscle tone, etc., as well as the presence of swelling or lumps anywhere on the body.

3. Increased or decreased water intake; increased intake can be a sign of kidney disease, and both increased and decreased intake are common signs of many infectious and other undesirable conditions.

4. Increased or decreased food intake; decreased intake is another very common sign of general illness or ill health; increased intake, if accompanied by no change in weight, can signal parasitic infestation.

5. Change in the quantity, frequency, and/or color of urine and urination; increased urination can be a sign of diabetes and other kidney or urinary-tract conditions; decreased urination can also be a sign of conditions affecting the urinary tract, including

or apathy, viciousness and general irritability can all be signs of ill health.

2. General physical deterioration, such as loss of

stones and cysts; a change in color or smell of urine can also signal disease, as well as nutritional deficiency.

6. Change in bowel excretion, either a change in the frequency of bowel movement or a change in the color or consistency of the excreted matter; diarrhea and constipation are among the most common bowel abnormalities, and both can be signs of disease and other poor conditions; excreta containing blood and/or mucous is cause for immediate concern and veterinary treatment.

7. Vomiting can be a sign of disease, poisoning, and many other conditions; a light case of vomiting may simply be the result a hairball or passing stomach upset, but chronic and/or severe vomiting, as well as bloody vomit, are all causes of immediate concern and veterinary treatment.

8. Weight loss, especially when accompanied by decreased activity, is a very common sign of illness; drastic weight gain can be a sign of hormone imbalance and other conditions.

9. Wheezing, coughing, sneezing, and other

*Take great care in protecting your cat from potentially dangerous objects.*

*If you acquaint yourself with the symptoms of illness in a cat, you can spare your pet—and yourself—a good deal of upset and anguish.*

breathing changes and problems are signs of ill condition; nose and eye discharge also signal poor health and deserve inspection.

10. Fever and chills almost invariably alert the owner to an ill condition in the cat; the cat's average temperature should typically range between 100.5°F and 102.5°F.

If your cat is suffering from an illness, it will very likely exhibit at least one of these ten key signs. Of course, these ten indicators are by no means the only signs of ill health, but they are the ten most common, universal signals for which the owner should be aware. Additionally, simply noting the presence of one of these signs is not the best way to incorporate them into your proper feline health keeping. It is always best to attempt to rule out all other possible causes before attributing the sign to disease, unless of course the condition requires immediate veterinary care regardless of the cause. Let us view a change in appetite as a less severe sign of illness: the owner may want to consider all changes in the environment (such as new pet introductions, children leaving home, etc.) as well as the consistency of affection bestowed on the cat in recent days. These and many other factors not related to disease could be the cause of the appetite change. And

*When clipping a cat's claws, take care not to cut the quick, the vein that runs through the claw.*

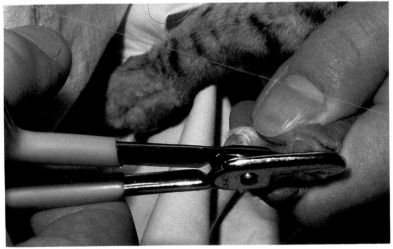

*A cat's paw pads should be checked periodically, especially if the cat spends time outdoors.*

treating the cat as if it were ill when in fact it simply required more affection or was experiencing an acclimatizing period with a new pet or without an old friend can further complicate the appetite condition. The responsible cat owner properly cares for his cat's health by noting the physical and temperament changes which occur in the cat, realizes the possible causes of these changes, and provide his feline charge with the appropriate veterinary and owner care.

## THE CAT'S TEMPERATURE

Taking the cat's temperature is very easy, provided a little cooperation is given by the cat. The average temperature of the domestic cat is about 101.5°F, with 100.5°F to 102.5°F considered normal. Fever is considered present when the cat's body temperature goes above 103°F, and chills are considered present when the body temperature falls below 100°F. The cat's body temperature is not constant, for daily, sometimes hourly, fluctuations occur. In general, the body temperature rises slightly during periods of activity and falls slightly during rest and sleep.

The cat's temperature is best taken with a feline rectal thermometer, available at a local pet shop or veterinary office. It is best to have someone to help you, holding and comforting the cat. The cat should be secured in either a lying or

*Cats are reasonably hardy animals; however, they can be subject to some serious illnesses and diseases.*

standing position. The cat's tail then should be held up, and about one-third of the rectal thermometer, lubricated with petroleum jelly, should be slowly inserted. The thermometer should be left in position for at least one minute, after which it can be gently removed and read.

## FIRST AID

All cat owners should have general knowledge of basic feline first-aid techniques and should have handy at all times a feline first-aid kit. The basics of a good first aid kit include antacids to relieve gastric upset and vomiting; anti-diarrhetics to treat simple diarrhea; antiseptic to clean minor wounds; bandages, cotton, gauze, and tape to cover minor wounds; hairball remedy; mineral oil to relieve constipation, protect the stomach lining, clean the ears, and treat hairballs; needlenose pliers and tweezers to remove foreign objects; rectal thermometer to monitor the cat's body temperature, and hand cleaner to sanitize your hands before (and after) treating the cat. The owner should consult a veterinarian regarding ideal products and dosage for his specific cat.

Regarding first aid techniques, the myriad of possible problems and the specifics of treatment for each of the many different conditions make impossible step-by-step instructions in a book of this size. The cat owner is encouraged to acquire the appropriate information through the purchase of a feline first-aid/medical text, free pamphlets offered by many companies and often available at veterinarians' offices, pet shops, and by writing to various organizations, and by attending seminars on cat health and safety.

## FELINE SAFETY

The age-old adage about a bit of prevention exceeding the value of a lot of treatment holds no truer than in providing a safe home environment for the cat to guard against accidental injury and death. Making the cat's home safe, commonly known as cat-proofing the home, is the first step in feline safety.

Cats are inquisitive creatures, and we all know another age-old adage about curiosity killing the feline. No doubt the cat can meet danger in any home: the most far-away loft, the most sealed-away closet, though forgotten by the owner, will be gladly explored by the cat. Open windows, hot stoves and burning pilot lights, open dryers and washing machines, oven cleaners, stain removers, detergents, and pesticides are but a few of the many common causes of injury and

*"What have we here?" Virtually every moving object is fair game for a cat.*

death to the cat. Reports indicate that many cats each year are trapped and killed in dryers and other household appliances. The owner must ensure that washers, dryers, refrigerators, dishwashers, and other appliances are kept securely shut and are checked for the cat's presence before their use. Electrical outlets and cords are also very real dangers to the feline. Houseplants, most of which are poisonous to cats, take many lives unnecessarily each year. Electrical outlets are best secured with a child-proof cover, and electrical cords should be hidden if possible. Cords which cannot be completely hidden can be coated with hot pepper or another deterring, non-toxic

*Common sense on the part of the cat owner can help prevent many a mishap.*

substance. Because so many houseplants are toxic to cats, the cat owner may be best not having live plants in the home; but, if plants are desired, they ought to be at least kept high out of the reach of the cat. Additionally, fallen leaves and pieces must be disposed of immediately. Other common poisons in the home include moth balls, paint thinners, human medications, and automobile antifreeze, to name but a few. Essentially, these facts and suggestions provide but a base of ideas from which the owner can cat-proof his home. Successful cat-proofing relies mostly on common sense and precaution. If there is any doubt that a substance, location, or other factor may be a a source of danger, the owner is encouraged to take the necessary precautions to prevent the cat's getting to or into it.